Sarah Orne Jewett

A Marsh Island

Sarah Orne Jewett

A Marsh Island

ISBN/EAN: 9783744724883

Printed in Europe, USA, Canada, Australia, Japan

Cover: Foto ©Thomas Meinert / pixelio.de

More available books at **www.hansebooks.com**

A MARSH ISLAND

BY

SARAH ORNE JEWETT

BOSTON AND NEW YORK
HOUGHTON, MIFFLIN AND COMPANY
The Riverside Press, Cambridge
1885

A MARSH ISLAND.

I.

ONE August afternoon the people who drove along the east road of a pleasant Sussex County town were much interested in the appearance of a young man who was hard at work before a slender easel near the wayside. Most of the spectators felt a strong desire to linger; if any had happened to be afoot they would surely have looked over the artist's shoulder; as it was, they inspected with some contempt the bit of scenery which was honored with so much attention. This was in no way remarkable. They saw a familiar row of willows and a foreground of pasture, broken here and there by gray rocks, while beyond a tide river the marshes seemed to stretch away to the end of the world.

Almost everybody who drove along would have confidently directed the stranger to a better specimen of the natural beauties of the town, yet he seemed unsuspicious of his mistake, and painted busily. Sometimes he strolled away, apparently taking aimless steps, but always keeping his eyes fixed upon the landscape, while once he flung himself impatiently at full length on the soft grass, in the shade of the nearest tree. One would have said that such enthusiastic interest in his pursuit was exceptional rather than common with him; but he presently took a new view of his subject from this point, and after some reflection rose and went nearer to a slender birch-tree which stood in his left foreground. There was a touch of uncommon color on some of its leaves, which had been changed early, and he held the twig in his hand, rustled it, and looked up at the topmost branches, which seemed all a-shiver at this strange attention. The light breeze passed over; the young tree was still again. A boy might have bent it, and cut and trimmed it with his jack-knife, for an afternoon's fishing, and the artist reached out and for a moment held the stem, which had lately put on its first white dress; then he let it spring away from him. Trees that grow alone have a great deal more individuality than those which stand in companies; the young man gave another look at the charming outline of this one, and went back toward his easel. As he turned he was suddenly attracted by the beauty of the landscape which had been behind him all the afternoon. The moorland-like hills were beginning to grow purple, and a lovely light had gathered into the country which lay between him and the western sky. He condemned himself for having been so easily suited with his point of view, and felt dissatisfied and displeased for the moment with his day's work.

At his feet grew an enticing crop of mushrooms, and with a sigh at the evasiveness of Art he stooped to gather the little harvest, and filled a handkerchief with the delicate pink and white fungi; tossing away the sunburnt ones of yesterday's growth, and biting two or three of the smallest buttons with a good relish. "If I only had some salt, now!" he said to himself. "I wonder what time it is;" then he looked somewhat eagerly along the road, as if he expected a companion.

Nobody could be discovered. It was some time since any traveler had passed that way;

the few wagons that had gone to market early in the morning had long since returned, and the greater part of the men and horses were busy on the marshes, — for this was the time of year for cutting the salt hay. When he looked at his sketch again it made him forget his other thoughts, and holding his brush at arm's length, and again stepping to and fro lightly, he put in some necessary touches with most delicate intention and pleasure. "Not so bad!" he said half aloud, "though my birch-tree does not look as if she could flit away if I frightened her, as the real one does."

There was a pervading flavor of idleness and of pleasure about the young man's industry. The olive-like willows and the birch-tree and the shining water seemed to lend themselves to his apparent holiday-making. Not a great distance away, the mowers wished it were still nearer sundown, as they went slowly back and forward on the marsh. This was a hot day for out-of-door work; the scythes could not be kept sharp enough, and the sun was dazzling everybody's eyes as it went down in the west. Even the good-natured jokes of some workmen could not shame away the frequent grumbling of others.

The artist could sometimes see the shine of a scythe, and hear a far-away peal of laughter or a shout, and this gave him a pleasant sense of companionship. He would have thought it was the charming weather that made him so happy and his work so prosperous if he had thought anything at all about it. He was too well used to good fortune to make any special note of this day, being endowed with a disposition which is not troubled by bad weather of any sort, and only waits, bird-like and meditative, to fly forth again when the sun is out. In fact, while the serenity of his personal atmosphere possessed a certain impenetrability for its enemies, friends could share it, and were attracted by the cheerful magnet at the centre. This young man had usually found his fellow-creatures wonderfully pleasant and ready to further his projects. He was called lucky, and sometimes selfish, by those who envied him, while his friends insisted that he gave them pleasure of the best and most unselfish sort. His virtues came of moral excellence, no doubt; still, the mysterious electric currents are at the root of our likes and dislikes. His nature was attractive, and everywhere admirers, and even friends, flocked to the standard of this curly-haired and cheerful knight, while one castle gate after another opened before him as he went his way through life. To be not uncomfortably young, to be boyishly hungry and enviably enthusiastic, to find the world interesting, and, on the whole, faithful to its promises, were happy conditions. A respectable gift for water-color painting and an admirable ambition to excel in the use of oil colors made sufficient business responsibilities. If sometimes existence seemed to lead nowhere in particular, and his hopes and projects were directed toward results too close at hand, it was because our hero felt an impatience for the great motive power of his life to take possession of him. He had a dim sense of his best self, as if it were a sort of spiritual companionship, and had once said that he believed he was waiting orders; confessing also that he had checked himself in various indiscretions, because he should not like to carry a bad record to his noble future. The friend who listened to this, being an older man, smiled under cover of the darkness, and called Dick Dale a girlish fellow, but a good one, before he laughed aloud, and wished him good fortune in a way that implied there was really no such thing.

Since advancement and glory are the reward of one's own definite effort, young Dale was as far as ever from possessing them. He was apparently unambitious, but his life was remarkably free from reproach, while he was often proved useful and always agreeable by his next neighbors. His smallest daily duties and pleasures were considered with increasing zest and respectfulness. Society valued him and instinctively paid him deference, as if it understood how sincerely he respected himself. He had often smiled when his fellows achieved early distinction and renown; if he had been poor, some croakers said, he would have made his mark, but those persons who knew him best laughed at the idea of its already being too late.

The day's work, or play, whichever it might have been, was finished, and, his excitement having fairly burnt itself out, the painter looked along the road eagerly, and began to put his brushes and colors together for transportation. Then he went to the top of a hillock near by, hoping to get a wider view of the vacant road. Afterward, resigning himself to patience and looking hopelessly at his stopped watch, he sat down for a quarter of an hour, and diligently tried to make a whistle from a willow twig; but the autumn bark proved disobligingly dry, and would not slip nor lend itself to sweet sounds.

The scythes had all disappeared from the distant meadow. It seemed at last as if our friend were left sole tenant of the country, for the sun was almost down, and the shadows were damp and chilly as they gathered fast in the low ground. He tried wistfully once or twice to see if a friendly haymaker could not be summoned. He grew more and more angry with the boy who had left him there late in the morning, with orders to come for him again at four o'clock. It appeared like a forsaken neighborhood, and Mr. Dale desperately climbed the shattered fence, and, having shouldered his artistic belongings as best he might, set forth with a limping gait toward the only house in sight. The road was perfectly level, and deep in white dust. The house looked a good way off; perhaps it was two thirds of a mile. The whole region seemed to be wild or reclaimed marsh land, except this farm, which covered a hill with its orchards and upland fields and pastures.

It was like a high, fruitful island in that sea of grass, the wayfarer thought; the salt inlets, indeed, surrounded it, though in some places one could leap the narrow ditches easily. The nearer he approached, the more picturesque and enticing he thought the farm. There was a great red barn well settled in the hillside, and a bluish-green company of willows, with some poplars and an elm or two, were clustered about the hospitable-looking dwelling. Pleasantest of all, at that moment, a straight plume of smoke was going up from one of the chimneys, most supper-like in its suggestion.

II.

The warm yellow glow of the sun shone out once more through the haze, and filled the orchard and all the shaded places of the Marsh Island with a flood of golden light. The apple-trees and the willows were transfigured for a few minutes, and as the young man saw a bright reflection on the window panes of the house he felt a great longing to paint the scene before him, and seized every possible detail of it with his delighted eyes. It did not seem so late, now that the sun was out again, and he turned once, a little reluctant, to look down the road; for he might have been too impatient for the coming of the boy.

The slow horse and rattling wagon were, happily, not approaching, and he assured himself that his only resource was the good-will of the farmhouse. Perhaps he could find shelter there for the night, and make another sketch in the morning. There was not a more picturesque bit of country in America!

Mrs. Owen, the mistress of this thriving homestead, came to stand in the doorway just at that moment, being influenced by the beauty of the sunset, yet not consciously recognizing the fact. She discovered her husband, who had left the marshes earlier than the rest of the mowers, standing still, half-way across the dooryard.

"You've had a good day's work, for such an old gentleman," she said, with affectionate raillery. "What are you a-watchin'? I declare, these trees have so overgrown we might's well live in the woods." But she noticed with considerable curiosity the pleased way in which the gray-haired farmer looked up through the topmost willow boughs to see the sunlight fade and disappear.

"'T was pretty, was n't it?" he answered. "I think the old place never looks so well as it does in one of these yaller, fallish sundowns."

"I thought it seemed clouded over a while ago," remarked the wife, after a moment's reflection, "but the sun must have burnt it off. I think likely you'll have another good hay-day to-morrow," and she took a shrewd look at the heavens wherever they were visible from the doorstep, and finally came forward, past the corner of the house, in order to get a fair look at the west. She was a round-faced, pleasant-looking woman, who had by no means lost all her youthful charms, though she stepped heavily, and was nearer sixty than fifty; one would have thought her much younger than her husband.

"Where's Doris?" he asked presently.

"Right up there in her room. She's been sewing on my new dress this afternoon. I thought likely it might come cool any day now, and I should need it. I told her I'd get supper, if she wanted to finish. Doris is one that does n't like to let the ends o' work lay over, just like me. And she's promised to be off this evenin'."

The farmer was beginning to ask a question, as they walked toward the door together, when his wife turned back at the sound of approaching footsteps. "Sakes alive, there comes a peddler!" she exclaimed. "You just tend to him, Isr'el. I must put the tea on; the men'll be here before we know it," and she hurried into the house to establish herself behind the nearest window blind, and make sure what the stranger and foreigner wished to offer before she allowed herself to be interviewed in person.

Doris also looked out of the window just above, at the sound of a strange voice. The young man carried a picture carefully in his hand, and a bundle of sticks and other paraphernalia beside. He was asking if he could be driven to the next town, or, better still, if he could have a night's lodging at the farm, and laughingly explained his forsaken condition. "I would have walked back, and thought nothing of it," he concluded, " but I was thrown from a horse not long ago, and I am a little lame yet."

"I'll speak to mother first," said the host. "She must have her say about keepin' ye;" but he was most favorably inclined toward the stranger, and called his wife, who waited a few moments before replying, and then took the farthest way, all round the kitchen, from her window to the door close beside it.

"This young man wants to know if you can keep him over night?" the farmer inquired, with a sort of appealing decisiveness, while Mrs. Owen, moved by proper wisdom, regarded the wayfarer with stern scrutiny. He was undeniably a gentleman, which was both an incentive and a shock to her housekeeping instincts. It involved the use of a spare bedroom and some difference in the supper; but after all, she might as well take the chance of good society and earning a dollar as anybody else. The poor fellow looked anxious, and with the air of granting a favor Mrs. Owen nodded and gave her permission.

There was a word or two of hearty thanks, as the stranger put down his burden; but the decision having been given, he seemed to become one of the household at once, and looked up at his landlady with a frank friendliness which brought a tinge of girlish color into her solid cheek. "Here are some mushrooms I found in the pasture," he said, and handed her the knotted handkerchief which had been slung to one of the rods of the easel.

Mrs. Owen looked doubtful, but pleased, and proceeded to examine them at once. "Dear me, I don't want none of them," she answered. "I should expect to be p'isoned, certain sure. Perhaps you're acquainted with them where you come from, but we don't eat such about here."

"Oh, but they're too good to be thrown away," protested the hungry young fellow. "I can cook them myself, if you don't mind."

"Bless you, lad, I'll get you a good supper, and welcome," announced Mrs. Owen, with an air of confidence in her own powers. " Doris, Doris ! " she called, lifting her face toward the upper window. " Won't you come down ? I 'll show you your room quick as I can," she added to the guest, as she disappeared within the door.

"' Doris?'" he repeated questioningly to the farmer, who had been listening with a pleased smile to the conversation. " What a pretty name ! "

" That 's my daughter, — all the girl we 've got," said Mr. Owen. "' *T is* a good name ; 't was my mother's, and her mother's before her. . . . What might I call you ? " was added presently, in a half-confidential way, though, to judge from the tone, the motive was interest instead of curiosity.

" Dale," answered the young man. " And you 're Mr. Owen, I believe. I asked that young scalawag who drove me over this noon. I noticed the farm when we were crossing the marshes."

" Isr'el Owen is right. I 'm owin' only in name, though ; " and the guest laughed promptly at the time-honored joke, and even gave an admiring glance at the comfortable old house and its surroundings. " We 'd better come in now; 't is getting damp. The women 'll show you a place for your picture. Well, that's very pretty, I declare," as it was turned into view. "I 'm glad I left that little white birch for ye. I was obliged to clear up the pasture some this last fall, but somehow or 'nother I did n't meddle with that. They 're tender-lookin' things, them little birches, though they 'll catch on to the rocks where nothing else will. The old willers, too, — you 've got 'em complete. Follow it for a trade, do ye?" But the answer seemed to be taken for granted, while Dick was wondering what he had better say.

The Owens' guest had made friends with many a country household, but this episode promised to be most charming, and an unreasonable satisfaction filled his mind at every new feature of such homely life. He had been graciously invited to step into the clock-room, and he could see through the gathering twilight an assemblage of old furnishings and a general aspect of rural dignity and self-respect. He was already impatient of his countrymen's habit of following a beaten track, having learned to travel more sensibly abroad. This was evidently the home of an old-fashioned farmer of the best sort, and Dick Dale became blissfully enthusiastic as he planned a short residence in such a delightful region. It seemed a great while since he had first driven along these roads, and made up his mind that some day or other he must come back quietly by himself to make some sketches. This was like a dream's coming true. He had just changed his plans on a sudden impulse, meaning to have only a day or two for himself before he kept a half engagement to join some acquaintances in town. Was not he his own master? And what difference would a delicious week or two here make to anybody but himself? He had a simple fondness for a summer's round of visits, and yet had persuaded himself lately that he was wasting his time. "How a fellow does tie himself hand and foot for six weeks together!" he sagely reflected. "This is like a bit of freedom," and he listened for a moment to the steady ticking of the monarch of the clock-room. It was a mere chance that he was here. The sketching of the day before had been unsuccessful, and he was blaming himself for his nonsense as he came away from the next town that very morning. He had after all taken hold of the golden string. The old farmer was a man of whom one should make the most. Once Dick had known another of exactly the same sort, in Devonshire; they might be brothers. And Doris, too, — there was Doris; the young man's heart gave an impatient bound. If she proved to be the flower of this fine old growth, his adventure would be worth having.

Somebody was stepping quickly about in the room overhead, but Mr. Dale at that moment ceased his vague anticipations, and went out, as if he were quite familiar with his position, to find Mrs. Owen in the kitchen.

"I s'pose you 're getting sharp set enough by this time," said the hostess; "but you make yourself at home, and I won't keep you waiting a great while. 'T is later than we commonly set down to supper, but when the men folks are getting in the salt hay it keeps everything at odds. Isr'el 's most through milkin', he says. He fetched the cows up early, but he come out, just as we saw you, to look an' see if the sun set all right. He 's too fanciful for such an old creatur', I tell him," and she looked up at the young man's face for the sympathy and intelligence she was sure to find.

"Oh, I'll make myself at home," Dale answered. "Something would happen to that boy if he came after me now. I should like very much indeed to stay a day or two here, instead of over night. It would be so near my — work."

"We shall have to think that over, I expect, — all of us," the busy woman answered, hurrying to the stove. "But you're welcome to-night, certain. There, Doris, you take Mr. Dale up and show him his bedroom, and we won't waste time on apologies, for you've got to take us as you find us."

A door had opened at the foot of a flight of stairs, and a tall young woman half withdrew in her surprise at meeting the stranger unexpectedly. It would not be proper to show him to his room except by the front staircase, and so she came down into the kitchen. "You will almost want a candle," she said, in a clear, fine voice, and led the way through the clock-room with perfect composure, and finally left him in a small chamber, whose single window was open to the faded western sky.

"Doris, Doris," the young man said to

himself softly. "She is something new; it is like finding a garden flower growing in a field."

The very twilight in the house had helped to make the sight of her surprising. She walked before him, slender and stately; there was a perfection about her which made him scornfully reflect upon the ill-development, the incompleteness and rudimentariness, of most members of the human race. He could hardly wait to see her again, and an eagerness to make himself attractive to her took possession of him. The natural reverence which a truly beautiful woman can always inspire was by no means wanting, and so sweet a mystery as Doris must be solved as soon as possible.

The lower room and the entry through which they had come had been dark, so that the stranger stumbled once or twice, to his great displeasure, and might at last have gone headlong into the little bedroom if Doris had not said, "Mind the step!" with an air of gentle patience. His guide left him at the door, and as he looked about the room he thought it quiet and orderly enough to have been her own. After the darkness they had just left it seemed well lighted by the sunset, which was now all faint rose-color and gray. There was a plump-looking bed, like a well-risen loaf, and a straight-backed chair or two, and a small three-cornered washstand, toward which his paint-streaked hands led him at once. He lifted the water-jug with admiration. It held very little, but it was of an adorable shape and quality of ancient English crockery, and he reminded himself that he might find a way through old Mrs. Owen's heart to her closets; for who knew what unappreciated treasures might be hidden away? Over the narrow mantel-piece there hung a sword, and, as well as the guest could see, an army commission or discharge in a simple frame. Perhaps Doris had lost a lover, and a thrill of sympathy filled this new admirer's mind; but on second thought he concluded that it was much better for him than her having a present lover. She seemed too young to have known much of the war, and this might have been the property of an elder brother or an uncle, or even the trophy of Farmer Owen himself. There was no reason why the sword should not have been there since the days of the Revolution, for that matter; the house was certainly old enough, and looked, so far as he had seen, as if there had been few changes during the last half century. There was a state of complete surrender to fate involved by the absence of any personal property, and after taking a long look from the narrow window, which made him more in love with the countryside than ever, Dick Dale attempted to return to the society of his new friends. A fear of lurking pitfalls of back staircases made him advance slowly, but with entire safety to himself. He thought once with great amusement that he was capable of making the most of a slight twist to his ankle in order to secure a week's stay at the farm. Art might be his excuse, at any rate, for he was quite sincere in wishing to carry away some sketches of the Sussex neighborhood. This was not a very purposeful young man: those who were growing old already among his comrades might laugh or scold at him for his apparent neglect of life's great opportunities, but nobody could accuse him of not making the most of the days as they came. His idleness might have made him wiser than their business had made them, but this was hardly proved to most people's satisfaction. If he did nothing for himself, a few had said sneeringly, everybody was the more ready to serve him. But the rest knew that he was only an idle hero, and loved him and believed in him, and had need of patience.

Downstairs in the kitchen Israel Owen and his wife had been discussing this interesting young man who had suddenly demanded their hospitality. Guests were by no means rare in summer weather, but the list of relatives and friends had been shortened in the last few years, and many of the old aunts and cousins had died who used to depend upon a visit at the farm. Doris was not one who made many acquaintances, her mother had often said, with regret. She had been sent to Westmarket to school, and stood well in her classes, beside having the advantage of good society at the cousin's house where she boarded; but she had seemed entirely contented to be at home ever since. Mrs. Owen possessed a most social nature, and always wished for more excitement and news than it was possible to find. She would have liked a village life best, with plenty of visiting from house to house and great authority in parish matters. She truly loved her husband, but when she married him it was with a firm determination to persuade him to sell the farm before many years, and the marsh island was but a stepping-stone for her ambition. She had stood there disappointed ever since, for the fancied stepping-stone had proved to be a pedestal. She had requested earnestly, in early life, that they might go to some centre of civilization, for the children's sake; but of late years, when Doris was found to be, as was often asserted, just such a slow-coach as her father, Martha Owen had resigned herself to her fate. Nobody knew better than she that she was looked upon with envy by all her neighbors. She had money enough and to spare, but for all that she was secretly grieved and dissatisfied because she spent her days as a farmer's wife. Her acquaintances were well used to her complaints. She was a cheerful, friendly soul, even in her fault-finding, and a listener was more apt to laugh at than to pity her smaller troubles. However, the undercurrent of dislike was sure to be felt by those who lived with her, and her family recognized a day now and then when it was best to step gently on their way, and not venture upon the discussion of even a trifling subject.

"He's no strolling fellow," she was saying of her guest. "You just look at that handkerchief with the toadstools in it. No finer linen ever came into this house. And even his initials on it, like a girl's. Most likely 't is some fancy led him here painting pictures. I don't believe he follows it for a trade, but he may. I wish I'd told him to throw these things out," she added, looking at the contents of the handkerchief with considerable awe. " I'll let him take care of 'em, any way. I don't want 'em round the kitchen."

" What's one man's meat 's another man's p'ison," sagely observed one of the young haymakers, who had drenched his head well at the pump, and sat fanning himself with his frayed straw hat on the doorstep. " I used to work over to the quarries with an old Frenchman, who pretty near lived on 'em while they lasted. He give me some one day on a piece of bread, and they tasted first rate. I never saw such a chowder as he could set on to the table. Did n't know what it was when he first caught sight of it, either."

" The French is born cooks, I 've always heard," said Mrs. Owen, not wishing to be instructed by this stripling, while her husband chivalrously resented so limited a view of the great nation, and said meditatively that he did n't doubt that Bonaparte could have cooked if he tried. He did everything else he undertook for a time.

"The boys used to rough that old fellow on account of eatin' frogs," Jim Fales asserted, as if he were determined to be the ally of his hostess. He was waiting impatiently for his supper at that moment.

"The young man spoke about bein' kept longer than over night, did n't he?" asked the master of the house softly, as if he favored the idea. "I declare, Marthy, he makes me think of Isr'el a little. He 's got a pleasant way with him. I don't know but what I should say yes; if you feel to, that is."

"We need n't urge him quick as he gets downstairs," came the answer from the pantry. "We 're noways obliged to keep boarders; and we 're a-cuttin' the ma'sh hay, that always makes extry work; and it 's inconvenient havin' Temp'rance off, though Doris and I get along well enough without her so far. I suppose he 'd be willin' to pay high board; but there, we may never hear nothing more about it. I do' know but what he does favor Isr'el a little about his forehead an' eyes," she added, in a lower tone. "Now,

Jim Fales, do call in Mr. Jenks and Allen, and have your supper. You 've been lookin' hungry enough at me to scare anybody, like the old cat yisterday, after she 'd been shut up in the apple sullar since Wednesday. She was follerin' me the whole forenoon."

"Where 's Doris ? " asked the farmer again. " Why ain't she helpin' of you ? "

" She 's had some supper, — all she wanted," replied the mother, bustling more than ever, and retreating to the outer kitchen, where the stove had its summer residence. " They 've got to git there earlier 'n common. This is the night she promised to go over to the minister's with Dan Lester. Some of the young folks " —

" That 's all right," and Mr. Owen's voice had a more satisfied tone than his wife's. " But I thought 't was Thursday nights they went. I forgot about the parson's being away this week."

" 'T would have been just as well for me if she 'd kept at home to-night, but I ain't one to complain. Dan Lester takes a good deal for granted lately, seems to me."

" He 's been working smart all day," said the farmer. " Dan 's a willin' fellow, and there were others knew that I was short of help. I 'd fetched him home to supper if I had remembered about to-night."

"He could n't ride over there with his haying rig on," replied the mistress, scornfully taking her place at the head of the table, and pouring a steaming cup of tea for anybody who would come to claim it. All the haymakers filed in at the door at that minute, and began to help themselves before they were fairly seated.

"I 'll speak to the young man," said Mr. Owen; but just at that moment the door opened, and Mr. Richard Dale made his appearance.

The three hungry men who had taken one side of the supper table to themselves paused for an instant to regard the stranger; then they all looked down again, and went on eating.

"You see we give you welcome to what we have, and make no stranger of you, my lad," said the master of the house, with fine old-fashioned courtesy; while Dale nodded and smiled, and began to prove himself as hungry as the rest.

"I hope I shall not frighten you, Mrs. Owen," he ventured to say presently, for there was a chilling silence upon the little company. "The truth is, I have had nothing to eat since breakfast;" at which the good woman's hospitable heart was touched, and she leaned over to see if his plate lacked anything. She had breakfasted before six o'clock, which was early enough at that time of year, when the mornings were much shorter than in June. Dale had had an advantage of three hours, or more, but the day since then seemed long; such a good supper as this was worth waiting for, and he stated the fact most sincerely. Soon the shyest member of the party was quite at his ease again, and the stranger was making each man his friend. His small adventure was rendered more amusing than it had really seemed at the time, and an ingenious threat and argument against the delinquent small boy served to entertain the company to such a degree that there was a merry shout of laughter. Jim Fales thought he had done this delightful companion a great wrong at first, and began to admire him intensely. The haymakers presently resumed a discussion of the probable length of a snake which had been seen at the edge of the marsh that day; but Mr. Jenks, the senior workman, continued to eat his supper, as if he considered that the most important duty of the moment. He resembled a sailor: there were small gold rings in his ears, and he had a foreign look, — acquired, it must have been, for he was unmistakably a New Englander to begin with. Dale soon found himself influenced by the deference which the rest of the party paid to Mr. Jenks, and looked up with pleased expectancy when the old farmer said, " Jenks, give us the particulars of that big raskill. You was one of three that killed him over on the Six-Mile Ma'sh. Don't set there lookin' as innycent as a man that 's drivin' a new hoss!" Whereupon silent Mr. Jenks was induced to tell his best story, though not without much precision and unnecessary delay.

It seemed very dark now, out-of-doors, and when some one drove quickly into the yard, toward the close of this unexpectedly festive occasion, the guest of the household felt a sudden dismay. He was enjoying himself with all his heart, and savagely assured himself that the boy might turn about and go back again. He would neither be driven into a ditch nor try to find his own way over unfamiliar roads.

Nobody seemed to be concerned with the

arrival, however, and our friend went on eating his hot gingerbread with its crisp crust. He observed that a shadow overspread Mrs. Owen's countenance for a moment, and presently took heart, and thought he need not have been so angry, after all. There was no sound of approaching footsteps, though he had distinctly heard some one leap to the ground; but directly the door at the foot of the stairway, which had received more than one hopeful glance, was opened, and Doris appeared again, ready for a drive. She was plainly dressed, and the second view of her was by no means disappointing. "I don't feel right to be leaving you, mother," she said, pausing a moment, " but I finished the dress." The elder woman hardly listened as she looked at her daughter with motherly pride, and then at the young stranger, who had risen and stood ready to escort Doris a little way; to open a door for her, perhaps, though the one which led to the yard was already open. He was strangely envious of the cavalier outside, and came quietly back to his place at the table. Everybody listened as the two voices — the girl's and was it her lover's? — exchanged greetings, and then the wheels trundled away down the road. The horse was not one that would stand well, but an excellent beast on the road, Mr. Owen at length mentioned, with a little reluctance at being obliged to speak first; and then there was another pause, and the crickets chirped louder than ever, and a rising breeze swayed the great willows and blew their faint fragrance through the wide kitchen.

Mrs. Owen had been embarrassed and a little flustered, as she would have expressed it, by the gallantry the handsome stranger had shown her daughter; the girl herself had accepted it without surprise. There was a charming dignity and simplicity about Doris, and if there were a chance, though Dick Dale was not experienced in figure-drawing, he would try to make a sketch of her, for her father's sake, before he went away. The old man's pathetic face grew more and more attractive to him, also, and altogether he was glad to be at the farm. He had not seen anything of such life as this since he was a boy.

III.

THE haymakers left their seats at the table, and strayed away one by one, and were seen no more that night. The day had been long and very hot for the season, and no doubt they were ready to seek their couches in the close, low-storied kitchen chamber. First, however, it was necessary to have a consultation upon the appearance of the stranger, and to make ingenious guesses at his past history, not omitting also his present circumstances and future plans.

"He never was this way before. Think likely he thought he 'd come round and take a look at the heathen," said Jim Fales, who was best acquainted in the neighborhood, and who, by virtue of a four months' residence in the family, could speak with great authority. His employer commonly asserted that James was young, but willing, when it became necessary to allude to him, and the haymakers themselves treated him with a cheerful forbearance which might easily have degenerated into something less. Jim had taken the place of a middle-aged man who had been Mr. Owen's mainstay for many years; but Asa had been persuaded, against the wishes and warnings of his Eastern friends, to join a brother who had long ago settled in the West. The haymakers asked Jim for news of him.

"Thought he'd grow up with the country, I expect," remarked Mr. Jenks, who was sitting at the end of the grindstone frame.

"Asa was well off," said Jim. "We think that his folks had an eye to his means, and expected, if they got him rooted up and planted out there, they could do as they were a mind to. I guess they'll have to set him out in a new spot before he'll shake down much of a crop of his dollars," the young man added smartly, much elated at his comparison.

"Asa was snug," agreed Mr. Jenks, not appearing to notice anything peculiar about the preceding statement. "I wa'n't what you would call well acquainted with him, but I guess he may make out to come back if he don't like. He never could have had no great expense here: he never had nothing special to lay his money out on, so 't was natural it accumulated."

"Some folks can't spend, and more can't save," said Allen, who was busily puffing at his pipe, which seemed to have some trouble with its draft. "They all seem to be openhanded, nice folks here to Owens'. Lord, what a supper I laid away! They live well, don't they?"

"Pretty fair," said Jim mildly, but with evident pleasure, as if he were being personally praised. His own clothes had grown very tight since he took up his residence on the Marsh Island.

It happened that Farmer Owen was also thinking of his own loss and Asa's lack of judgment. He and young Dale sat together in the side doorway, in two of the kitchen chairs, while the mistress of the house clicked and rattled the supper plates, and eclipsed the bright light of the kitchen as she went to and fro. Dick was listening to the crickets and the soft sounds that came out of the warm darkness, when Mr. Owen asked whether he had ever been much to the westward.

"Only once, a good while ago," he answered, a little surprised. But this seemed somewhat unsatisfactory.

"I've been wanting to inquire," said the farmer. "This region never was great for havin' the Western fever, but Asa Bunt, that has lived with us a good many years, — since my father's day 't was, — took a notion to seek his fortune. I guess a pack o' hungry, worthless folks o' his was seekin' theirs; they give him no peace."

Dale did not find himself deeply interested in this statement, and there was a short period of silence.

"My father's brothers and my mother's folks all followed the sea," said Israel Owen presently, "and I think my boy had it in him, for all I dwell so much upon having had him spared to be at home with me."

The listener turned his head, as if eager to know the rest of the story.

"Killed in the war, — all the boy I ever had," was the response. "Only twenty-one, he was, the April before he died in July. Shot dead, so he did n't suffer any, so far as we know. He's laying out here in the orchard, alongside the rest of the folks. I went out South and fetched him home to the old place. I've been thinking ever since I see you that you favor him in your looks: there's something about your forehead and eyes and the way your hair grows. I'll show you a likeness of him in the morning: 't is a rough thing that was taken in camp, that he sent home to me. There are some other pictures of him that his mother keeps, taken younger, but I seem to set the most by mine."

"That was his sword in the room I am to sleep in?" asked Dale, filled with pity, and understanding the pathetic smile of this apparently prosperous man.

"Yes. The folks thought they ought to have it down in the best room, but I did n't seem to want to. That was always his bedroom, and there are some other things there that belonged to him, and I like to keep 'em together. He was first leftenant when he was shot. There were two girls between him an' Doris, but they died very small. Doris is — I could n't get along without her nohow; but there 'd been an Isr'el Owen on the farm for near two hundred years, and now there 'll never be another. I ain't a sound man myself, so I was n't out in the army; but I never felt so cheap in my life as I did the forenoon I see Isr'el marchin' by, an' the rest of 'em. I never got no such news as when I heard he was shot. I've kep' the farm goin' and stood in my lot an' place the best I could, but I tell you it took the heart right out o' me."

Dale was silent; there was nothing he could say. The father had looked his sorrow in the face so long that a stranger's thought of it was not worth expression. Yet he could just remember his own father, and somehow a deep sympathy flashed quick from one man's heart to the other.

"You spoke about stopping in the neighborhood for a few days?" the host said, after a pause, in which they had both listened to the far-away strange cry of a sea-bird down on the marshes. Dale responded with instant gratitude and hopefulness: —

"I should like it very much. I must finish the picture I began to-day, and I wish to make several other sketches. It really would be a great favor if Mrs. Owen could make room for me. I must bring my traps over from Dunster, though. Will any of your people be driving that way in the morning?"

Mrs. Owen herself was standing near, and answered this, as if she were the only one to be consulted in such important arrangements. "We never have taken folks to board," she replied, " but I don't know as we ought to refuse you, — on Bible grounds," and she laughed good-naturedly.

" I am afraid you will be disappointed if you hope for an angel˙ this time," Dale smiled back again. He was standing in the doorway, and the light from the kitchen shone full in his handsome, boyish face. The farmer sighed, and leaned forward a little as he looked at him wistfully. But Martha Owen hastened to say that Doris was going to Dunster in the morning to have the colt shod, and as likely as not would be glad of company. The men folks would all be off about the salt hay.

Later that evening Dick Dale lay in bed listening again to the crickets, which kept up a ceaseless chirping about the house, and to the sober exclamations of the lonely sea-bird in the low land, not far away. The window was wide open, within reach of his hand, and once or twice he raised himself on his elbow to look up at the stars, which were gleaming and twinkling in a white host, whose armies seemed to cover the sky. The willows reached out their huge branches and made a small cloud of dense darkness, and the damp sea air was flavored with their fragrance and that of the newly mown marshes. There were no sounds, except those made by the faintly rustling leaves and the small chirping creatures, which seemed to have been stationed by the rural neighborhood as a kind of night watchmen to cry, All's well, and mark the time. The great loon was the minute-hand, while the crickets told the seconds with incessant diligence; as for the hours, they seemed so much longer than usual that whether a wind or a falling star announced their close it would be impossible to determine.

Since Israel Owen had made known the history of his dead son, the narrow chamber had become much more interesting. The present tenant of it was usually given to keeping late hours, but he had offered no objection when his host suggested that it was time to go to bed, feeling that it would be impossible to disregard the customs of the family that night, at least. Farmer Owen lingered a moment after he gave the young man a candle in a saucer candlestick, and looked at him as if he wished to say something. He was apparently unable to suit himself with words, however, and turned away with a cheerful "Good-night to ye, my lad;" but the short silence was not unmeaning. The candle had an unpleasant odor, and burned unevenly, letting a small torrent of its substance descend upon the well-brightened brass. Dick wondered, as he stood before it with his hands in his pockets, if Mrs. Owen would consent to part with the old candlestick; he thought it would look well in the studio which he occupied somewhat irregularly with a friend.

There was a square spot of glimmering white on the blue homespun covering of the bed, which proved to be a garment of primitive construction, and Dick inspected it with some amusement, until the thought struck him that it might have been part of the wardrobe of the young soldier. There was a mingled odor of camphor and herbs, as if it were just taken from a chest that was seldom opened. After a moment's reflection he shook it outside the window, and waved it to and fro gently in the mild night air. Then he proceeded to make a circuit of the room, and held the candle high while he read the lieutenant's commission. Dick had been much too young to go to the war himself, though he was thwarted in a fierce ambition to march afield as drummer-boy, and he felt a curious interest in the farmer lad to whom this cheap-looking bit of paper certified a place in history. Only one name among thousands, to be sure, but a name forever kept by his country! A thrill went through the man who read. He was much older than this Israel Owen, but he felt immeasurably younger. There was a dignity and pathos about the unused bedroom, though its present occupant looked round it next to see if there were anything else which it would be possible to read for an hour. A person who was by no means used to early hours could not help feeling wide awake at a little past nine. He had given Farmer Owen his last cigar, as they sat together in the doorway, and was thankful it was a good one; as for his cigarettes, they had failed altogether some hours before. Presently the feeble candle was out, and after the smoke of it had been blown away, and the clean, quiet place seemed only a protected corner of the wide, starlit world, he laughed a little at the unexpectedness of the situation, and then thought, with a shadow of envy, of Doris and the young man, and began to listen for the sound of returning wheels.

To-morrow would be Saturday; he must make the most of it. This would be pleasant enough to look back upon; but such a thin pillow and thick bed were worse than the bare ground. The confession must be made, however, that when Dan Lester, the enviable gallant, had helped his companion to descend from the new light carriage, which had been bought chiefly with a view to her pleasure, it was only twenty minutes to ten o'clock, and Mr. Richard Dale was already sound asleep.

IV.

As Doris and her cavalier turned out of the yard and drove down the road, they were both silent for a minute or two. The evening was very dark, and Doris lost all thought of her companion as she instinctively assumed a certain responsibility and kept watch before her. In a little while, however, her strong eyes became independent of the shadows, and as the horse's feet struck the smooth track of the highway she leaned back in the carriage, and her attention became diverted to the interests of the occasion. Dan Lester was a dim figure at her side; he had seen his way all the time and felt no uneasiness, and now turned to look at Doris with entire satisfaction. He knew perfectly well that nothing served his purpose better than to be able to claim Doris's companionship on the slightest pretext. Doris herself was so shy of lovemakers that he did not mean to startle her by any premature avowal of his true affection for her. This very evening his heart gave a happy beat, as he told himself that she could not have gone to the village very well without him; indeed, she might have to give up more than one pleasure if he were not always ready and glad to serve her; some day she would surely find out that she could not get along without him any better than he could without her. And the good fellow leaned over and smoothed the lap-robe, and tucked it in more closely. Most of the maidens whom he had known were willing to be agreeable, and to smile upon him and his attentions, and he was not averse to being smiled upon; but Doris Owen's lack of self-consciousness and quiet dignity attracted him, and kept him eager to follow and to win her. He could not remember a time when he did not feel for her a tenderness that nothing should change. To-night he reassured himself that at last he was able to marry a wife whenever he chose, and suddenly found it more difficult than ever to bide his time. Dan was quite aware that the neighbors had long ago ceased to feel any excitement about so natural and proper a match; they had talked it over and over, and settled his future for him, and even spoken to him on the subject without the least hesitation. But, strange to say, in these days, when he continually told himself that all obstacles had been removed, the lover became for the first time disturbed and uncertain. Doris was so friendly and sisterly, and unlike other girls who thought of marriage. Yet it was not impossible that she was quiet and sweet, and untroubled even by love; and Dan Lester grew scarlet all at once in the sheltering darkness, because he was possessed by an eager desire to risk asking the great question that very night. Perhaps Doris was waiting for him to declare himself; was wishing to hear the words he found it so hard to say.

At that instant the girl herself spoke, and he was instantly possessed by a sense of disappointment; there was evidently a complete unconsciousness of such an exciting possibility. "I was not sure that you would come," she said. "I hope you didn't feel obliged to keep the promise, if you were tired. I wasn't counting on it greatly, and haying is hard work."

Lester laughed uneasily. "'T would take more than haying to beat me," he answered, and touched his horse unnecessarily with the whip, after which his thoughts returned to a subject which had provoked his curiosity while he waited in the farmhouse yard. "Have you had company come?" he asked. "I saw a stranger at supper with the rest of the folks."

Doris was glad to have a new topic for conversation suggested. She half feared that it was an unwelcome tax upon Dan to drive her to the village that evening. He was unusually silent, and she had begun to be the least bit uncomfortable.

She hoped that he would not feel bound to her, yet her woman's heart had become aware that one element in their relation to each other was fast growing more conspicuous than any other; and she had lately both dreaded and enjoyed being alone with him. Dan had been her brother Israel's crony, and was a near neighbor. It was perfectly natural that he should be at the farm often.

"Mother told me that the young man's name is Dale," she answered, cordially. "I don't know anything about him, except that he was painting a picture somewhere near here to-day, and they forgot to come for him from Dunster; so he came up to the house, and asked to stay over night. They think he looks a good deal as Israel did," Doris added softly. "Father seemed to want him to stay. I did n't like to come away and leave mother with so much to do, but this morning she was very anxious to get word to Temp'rance; we were to let her know when we began to get the salt hay in. Mother said a little while ago that perhaps we 'd better let her stay another day or two, or go over to-morrow and get her; but I was afraid she would be all tired out. You know what mother is when there 's a great deal extra to do."

Dan Lester eagerly insisted that Doris had done exactly right. He had quickly understood Mrs. Owen's change of opinion, and found it enough to rouse a flame of jealousy. "Temp'rance has been away most a fortnight," he remarked as quietly as he could. "She never gets any rest over at her sister's, any way."

He could not be sufficiently thankful that Doris was not at home that evening, being suspicious of the unknown rival, and unpleasantly sure that Mrs. Owen was filled with ambitions for her daughter's future that overtopped and slighted his own claims. There was something ominous in the stranger's appearance at this critical time, and poor Lester wished that he were already sure that Doris belonged to him; he must settle it right away. But while he tried to gain courage to speak to her, Doris, who was in uncommonly good spirits, talked about one every-day thing after another until they reached the minister's door.

When the choir-meeting was over, fate would insist that a cousin, who lived half a mile or more beyond his own house, should ask to make a third passenger homeward in the new buggy. Dan was amazingly ungracious for the first few minutes, but the girls, who were good friends, gossiped together serenely all the way.

V.

THE various excitements of the evening apparently exhausted Mrs. Owen's reserve fund of good-humor, for she came downstairs the next morning looking older than usual and very despondent. Her husband, on the contrary, was in a cheerful frame of mind, and even hummed a tune as he waited for his breakfast. Whenever his companion had occasion to go to the kitchen closet, just behind the chair where he sat, she gave a deep and ostentatious sigh. The farmer was always an early riser, and had already fed the horses and cattle; he asked now, with mild interest, if none of his assistants had yet appeared.

There was no answer to such an unnecessary question, and a vague thought flitted through the good man's mind that perhaps this had been one of the idle words for which he must give account. It was hardly a rebuke to himself, but rather a theological view of an unimportant mistake. He still waited patiently, giving his best attention to his interlaced fingers, matching one thumb to the other, and wondering, also, what "mother" had on her mind now. He had known these signs of storm to precede even so reasonable an event as her going to the village to pay an afternoon visit, and a general overturning of affairs always preceded the more serious enterprise of deciding upon new clothes. He assured himself that the clouds were likely to blow over, and smiled suddenly at his own philosophy. It was half-past five o'clock; the morning was chilly and misty, and would have promised to an inland farmer anything but a good hay-day.

The smile reflected from his observation of the in-door weather seemed to deepen Mrs. Owen's sense of displeasure. "I'm getting the breakfast ready as fast's I can," she said, in a most offended tone. "You just try to do all your farm work with one pair o' hands, and see how you make out."

"I did n't know as anybody was ever in the habit of usin' two pair," suggested Israel Owen mildly. "None of us is expected to do any more than we can do. Don't overtax yourself, Marthy," he added, placidly. "I declare, I don't know when I've ever been so sharp-set for breakfast, though. I think most like it may be on account of the weather's being cooler. What's goin' on with you to-day? I hope Temp'rance 'll get home good an' early."

" 'T will be the first day since she's been gone that she could wear her new thick dress. I told her 't was all nonsense to toil so over it. Anybody might know 't was like to be too warm weather to have any good of such a thick material. She thought she'd have it ready for winter if she got it done now, in leisure time, before we begun to get the ma'sh hay in. An' she did n't have a notion that you would begin till Monday. I must say I hate to spoil her visit, sending and getting of her home."

"We're going over on the south ma'sh," said the farmer, tilting his chair, "and most likely won't be back before seven or eight o'clock. You might take the old horse and jog up Dunster way, and fetch Temp'rance home yourself, — 't will be a change."

The cause of Mrs. Owen's despondency was at once apparent, and the discovery of her plan seemed to excite great anger: "I'd just like to know how I'm going over there without a decent thing to wear over my shoulders. Nobody would expect that I belonged to folks who had means. I've got some pride, if you ain't. There's Temp'rance's folks from the West all there. I do consider they are weak about dress, and lo'd on too much of it without respect to occasion: but I don't feel happy when I've got nothin' to wear over me except old things that's only fit, and ought by good rights to be took, for rug-rags."

"They used to tell a story — I do' know but you've heard it — about old Sergeant Copp an' his wife, that was always quarrelin'," said the farmer, in a tone of great satisfaction. "Somebody heard her goin' on one day. Says she, 'I do wish somebody 'd give me a lift as fur as Westmarket. I do feel 's if I ought to buy me a cap. I ain't got a decent cap to my back: if I was to die to-morrow, I ain't got no cap that's fit to lay me out in!' 'Blast ye!' says he, 'why did n't ye die when ye had a cap?'"

Martha Owen tried to preserve her severe expression, but began to laugh in spite of herself, and her companion knew that this was an end of present discomfort. "It's your own fault if you an' Doris don't have what you want to wear," he added. "I'm sure I always make you free to spend what money you need, but you 're always a-sufferin' for somethin'."

"Well, there, it's more the trouble of gettin' clothes than anything else," said the good woman. "I s'pose I can go over an' get Temp'rance. We 'll have an early dinner soon as Doris gets back from Dunster with the young man. I shall have to send her off soon as we get breakfast cleared away," said the crafty mother. "There won't be a bit of tea in the house after tomorrow morning. We shall use up a sight with the three men, and now I suppose we must keep this new one. I don't know as he will make much trouble. They used to think Doris had a pretty taste for drawing; perhaps he will give her some lessons."

"He won't stay here long, at this time of the year," said the father. "We don't know a word about him, neither. I don't expect there 's anything wrong in him; he could n't look ye so straight in the eye. Doris ought to be coming down; it ain't usual with her to be so behindhand;" but at that minute her footfall was heard on the stairs.

Israel Owen's face brightened as he saw his daughter. "I thought 't was about time for you," he said affectionately.

Doris looked up at the clock, and then smiled at him without speaking.

"I don't know but quarter to six is full early enough," he answered. "I think hired men are apt to take it out in nooning, if they don't loiter all through the day, when you try to start 'em out too early. Your mother here has been hard at it since a little past five, though;" and this seemed like an attempt at reproach.

If Mrs. Owen had been allowed to speak her sorrows first, she could have made good use of the occasion; but as it was, she instantly defended her daughter, though in a manner which let both her companions understand that Doris had something else to answer for.

"You could n't have done anything until now, unless it was to open the fore-room windows before the young man comes down," she said; but after a minute's reflection and a glance at her father, Doris fell into line with the usual preparations for breakfast, and by six o'clock the family had assembled round the table. The sun had broken through the morning mists, and the kitchen seemed a very comfortable and smiling place. The company was much more prosaic and business-like than it had been the evening before, at supper-time, for the beginning of a busy day has not the leisure that the close of it offers as part of the worker's reward. Yet there has been a certain spirit of adventure at every breakfast table, whether it were surrounded by knights who were eager for the tournament, or bronze-faced haymakers ready to prove their prowess with the armies of straight-stemmed marsh grasses. The evening ought to find men tired, and it may find them disappointed and defeated; in the morning success seems possible, for who knows the treasures and surprises a new day may hold in its keeping?

As Dick Dale came through the clock-room he found the damp morning air very pleasant. There was no chill; only a sharp freshness, that gave an additional spur to his cheerful readiness to meet the world. The old farmer had opened the windows himself, and a straying branch of the cinnamon rose-bush outside had been turned by the light wind, and was lying across one of the window sills, as if it were eager to come inside. The young man crossed the room quickly as he heard the sound of voices, and paused for a minute on the threshold of the kitchen, held by a pleased artistic sense. He had become somewhat familiar with such rural interiors in England and France, but the homelike quality of this, the picturesque grouping and good coloring, were a great surprise and satisfaction : he noted the bronzed faces of the men, the level rays of the pale sunlight, the dull gleam of the brass mountings of a chest of drawers at the shaded side of the room, and the central figure of the girl, who brought a tall coffee-pot with both hands, as if it were an urn of classic shape. Her delicate features and clear color seemed to intensify themselves as he looked, — Doris would make a picture by herself. He must surely do the best he could at making a sketch of her.

Mrs. Owen thought the guest was experiencing an attack of awkwardness, and was not sure of his place at the table, and at once signified the seat which had been given him the evening before. After a few minutes the interruption was forgotten, and the regular progress of the breakfast went on, as if it had been a brook into which somebody had lately thrown a stone. Dale was half amused and half gratified with his new position. He had felt very much like other people until the evening before, but so sensitive a nature was aware that it had suddenly become the most interesting fact to several minds; that he represented an only half-understood order of things, and was looked upon with mingled suspicion and envy. It was not beyond his power to make his common humanity more apparent than the difference in experience and local values. Being, indeed, a man who was not ruled by the decorations of character, he had a true sympathy with his fellows, which gave him the advantage of feeling at home in almost any place; and with another glance at Doris, who sat by his side and next her father, without a word of entreaty to his companions, he began to lay the best claim he could to equal rights with the rest of the household. Busy Mrs. Owen could hardly spare time for her morning meal, and presently bustled away into the pantry to finish packing the dinner baskets. The farmer laid down his knife and fork, next, and carried the cider jug to the cellar, protesting that he had nearly forgotten it, which made the company smile; and two of the haymakers nodded at each other and grinned a moment later, when they heard their favorite beverage gurgling from its cask in the depths below. Then they went out together. There were a few reproachful cries at a restless horse, and a hurry and clatter and general excitement in the yard. The farmer came back again to the door to say that he should have to leave Mr. Dale to the favor of the women folks; but if he felt like strolling over to the marshes by and by he could find a welcome, especially if it looked like rain. The stranger himself laughed in response, and in a few minutes the stir was over, and quiet had again settled down upon the house. After a minute's hesitation Dick wandered back into the clock-room, and stood before the sketch he had made the day before. This was disappointing, after all; the little birch-tree was more like a tree and less like Doris than he had hoped to find it. Yet he was not sure that he felt exactly like going on with that bit of work; perhaps it would be better to look about the farm, and see what he could discover in the way of subjects. He had found his room at the north side of the house a little damp and cheerless that morning, and had doubted whether it were worth while to linger long in this rural neighborhood; but all trace of such want of hardiness had been dispelled by his comfortable breakfast. It really seemed his duty to forget inconveniences which could not be worth mentioning beside those he had encountered elsewhere in pursuit of his art. One did not happen upon such rich hunting-grounds every day, and he gave a complacent glance at a Washington pitcher of most rewarding quality, which held some durable dahlias and late sumner flowers, on the narrow table under the blurred mirror in its twisted frame. He was a trifle ashamed of his grasping worldliness, as he stood in the old room. The master of the house was most attractive; he and his daughter were of a different fibre from the other inmates of the household. The girl had a fine repose and dignity of manner. She seemed equal to her duties, but she was grave and brooding; like some women whom he had known among the French peasants, with her serene expectancy and steadfastness and careful expenditure of enthusiasm. She was an economist by nature, but rich with power and strength, the young man thought, as he wondered if there were any one who had the gift of sounding the depths of her faithful heart.

He was ready to read much romance and sentiment between the straight, plain lines of this new character. Evidently nothing of any great interest had happened to Doris yet, but it could not be possible that she was made only for fading out and growing old, undeveloped by these dull fashions of country life.

As he went up the broad green sloping yard toward the orchard, a little later, Mrs. Owen's voice reached him as she sang a high droning psalm tune behind the wilted scarlet runners of the pantry window. She had sung in the church choir in her early years, and had agreed with her neighbors that her gift was quite uncommon; but it was impossible now for the listener to resist a smile at some of her ambitious excursions among the higher notes. She was rolling out a new supply of the substantial ginger cakes that her dependents so much admired, and doughnuts also must be provided afresh; but she noticed with pleasure that her guest was going in the same direction from which Doris would presently be returning, and rejoiced to think they were sure to meet.

Nothing would give her daughter a better suggestion than such an acquaintance as this.

It was Mrs. Owen's darling project that Doris should see something of the world. She dimly recognized that the world had a claim upon the girl's beauty and good sense, and she wished to hear her praised and see her take a rightful place. Her own most womanly perception had not been unconscious of young Dale's interest in her child's good looks. Dale himself was pleasant to look at; young Israel Owen might have truly been something like him, if he had grown older under such evidently prosperous worldly conditions; and the tears started to this mother's eyes, as she watched the stranger out of sight. She must ask him some time to give further particulars of the accident which had lamed him. He seemed to have difficulty in using his left foot, and limped a good deal now as he disappeared among the old trees of the orchard. Presently he came into view again, this time allured to the family burying-ground at the edge of the field. The good woman could see, as he had seen, the faded color of the little flag which since the last Decoration Day had fluttered in every breeze above the soldier's grave.

VI.

THE weather did what it could to prosper the dwellers on the Marsh Island, and Dick Dale more than once assured himself that it was too heavenly beautiful for a man to do anything but enjoy life in idleness. There was a sturdiness and royalty about the stout-stemmed fruit-trees. He looked along delightful vistas between their rows, and when he had followed the hillside a short distance he discovered, as he turned to look behind him, a view of the farmhouse roofs and chimneys against the willows, with a far distance of shore and sea and clouds beyond, which appeared to him of inestimable beauty and value. He forgot, as he looked across the country, that he had ever known any interest in existence save that connected with his paints and brushes, and would have hurried back for the best of them if he had not remembered, almost with impatience, that Doris would be ready to drive him to Dunster at eight o'clock. It was now a little past seven, and there never had been a better beginning of a day, with such wealth of time yet to look forward to. If Dale had been a more energetic person, he might have seized that perfection of morning light, and made sure of his sketch directly; but he looked back lovingly again and again instead, was sorry that the family plans seemed too important and inevitable to be disarranged, and strolled on through the open field. The aftermath here was wet with the heavy dew of the night before, and he kept to the cart track, along which the workmen had evidently passed earlier in the day. One of the ruts was well trodden and much used as a footpath. He wondered whither it led: it must be to the creek, and there was sure to be a fine view of the marshes after one reached the top of the slope beyond.

A salter breeze than any he had met blew the drier grasses of the hill-top, and for his lame foot's sake he stopped, and then looked about eagerly. A wide, low country stretched away northward and eastward, with some pale blue hills on its horizon. The marshes looked as if the land had been raveled out into the sea, for the tide creeks and inlets were brimful of water, and some gulls were flashing their wings in the sunlight, as if they were rejoiced at the sight of the sinking and conquered shore. The far-away dunes of white sand were bewildering to look at, and their shadows were purple even at that distance. One might be thankful that he had risen early that morning, and had climbed a hill to see the world. Far away the haymaking was going on. In another direction some old haystacks looked soft and brown; and then Dale discovered a second group of men floating down the creeks, and was puzzled to know which were his friends. He felt like a leaf that drifts down a slow stream; he grew serenely contented in his delight, and dared to look the August sun full in its face, and then threw a stone with all his might at a bird that flew by. He blinked his dazzled eyes angrily because he could not tell whether the shot had been of any avail, and then laughed at himself, and felt like a boy on a stolen holiday. Just then he heard a noise of heavy footsteps, and behind some bushes, farther along the path he had been following, he was surprised to see Doris approaching, walking quickly beside two farm horses, whose harness was hanging about them, unfastened and clinking as they came. She was holding the near horse by his bit, and leaned backward to check the honest creatures, who were impatient to finish their breakfasts. The color flickered more brightly in her cheeks as she saw Dale, and watched him eagerly come down the slope to meet her.

The clumsy horses were filled with the spirit and excitement of the clear morning, and were ready to take advantage of any excuse for prancing a little. They raised their heads and looked at the stranger, and the off horse capered at the sight; the dangling harness struck them unexpectedly, and their slender teamster was suddenly in danger. At least, Dale thought so, and hastened to the rescue. Doris lost sight of him, but presently had the horses well in hand again, and a moment afterward she was shocked to see the painter try to get up from the turf. He had stumbled and fallen ignominiously, but looked pale, as if he were really hurt. The conquered horses stood still now, at the girl's command. They were docile creatures, of great experience, who would stand in the hot sunshine all day, or follow the long spring furrows without impatience. They would not have struck their young mistress for all the cracked corn in the bin, and waited now, looking after her uneasily as she went toward the stranger.

"It is only this confounded ankle of mine!" growled Dale. "I believe I never shall get it strong;" and though he felt more and more disgusted and ashamed of himself and wished he were a thousand miles away, an unpleasant faintness was creeping over him. No, he would not be such a baby! But at this point the bright sky turned black, he felt the ground lift itself up and the short grass prick his cheek, and there was a pause altogether.

Only a minute went by before life resumed its course, and he opened his eyes, quite a languid and white-faced person now, instead of the stalwart admirer of the country who had come up the hill. "You had better lie still a little while," said Doris softly. He need not have felt such a sense of inferiority and silliness, for her face was very sober and distressed. The horses had become totally indifferent to their surroundings, except as they tried to brush away a fly now and then. Dale sat up presently, and leaned his head on one hand while he felt his disabled ankle with the other, and then tied his handkerchief tightly about it. He felt sorry it was not the clean one which he had filled with mushrooms the day before; this looked miserably the worse for wear. Somehow, he never could remember to beg for paint rags before he started out for a day's sketching.

Doris looked on compassionately. She was standing close beside him, and he was sure she had stooped to take off his hat, which had been uncomfortably misplaced over his eyes as he lay down; but she had not lifted his head on her arm, or behaved at all as maidens do when their lovers, or even their friends, faint in the story-books. He was obliged to confess that she was very sensible and very kind, however, and that she looked sorry for him.

"I shall be all right directly," he said, with his best smile. "I must insist that I have n't fainted before since I was a boy. Could you ask" — and Dale hesitated: there was nobody at the farmhouse save Mrs. Owen. "Can you get me a stick, do you think, so that I can hobble back to the house?"

"I will come back and help you, if you will wait right here for me," said the girl, flushing slightly, while, leading the horses the side of the path, she sprang upon the back of the nearer one, and went jolting

toward the barns with entire composure.
She was apparently familiar with this uncomfortable mode of travel; she did not turn her head, though Dale turned his, and saw her strike first the leader and then his mate with the end of the heavy leather reins. He wondered if she would not be hurt against the low boughs of the old apple-trees; he had been obliged to stoop more than once as he had walked under them. It was very odd that he should have been talking nonsense to himself the night before about being invalided upon the Marsh Island. Somehow, the reality was not so pleasant, and he felt like a shipwrecked sailor, and unwontedly destitute at that. He could not go to Dunster now; perhaps he must ask Doris to bring a doctor. This was a dismal end to his triumphant morning; but his ankle was in a wretched way, and with an angry cry of misery, which nothing would have forced from him had he not been alone, he seized it with both hands, and soliloquized at intervals until Doris reappeared. Even in his suffering condition he felt a great joy, because she ran so lightly and so fast, as not one woman in ten thousand can run, with fleet-footed directness and grace. She was slow, she her-

self thought, — she had been afraid that he might faint again; and when she reached his side, and Dale leaned upon her firm arm and stopped to break a stick from a wild-cherry thicket, she thought him uncomplaining and even heroic. She was much disturbed, but the painter thought her very placid and quite motherly in her attentions and feeling toward him. She was a soulless creature, after all; beautiful to look at as a fawn and unconscious as a flower, but as a human being utterly commonplace. The confession must be made that when they reached the hot kitchen, and Dale deposited himself wearily in a padded rocking-chair, which he wished to be out of directly, Mrs. Owen was much more equal to the occasion in her expressions of sympathy than her daughter had been. "For mercy's sake, Doris," she demanded, "why did n't you slip one of the hosses into the old wagon, and not make Mr. Dale walk all the way? He may have het up the bone so 't will be stiff as a stake." But Doris looked so convicted and distressed that Dick announced gallantly his complete repugnance to being cruelly jolted over the uneven surface of a hillside field.

Dan Lester was happily unconscious of the devotion which was spent upon his rival that day at the farmhouse. The family doctor was seen coming along the road, and was called in with great eagerness. He looked at his patient with much surprise, and recognized him as having sometimes been a guest at one of the fine houses on the shore, at the other extremity of his range of practice. The doctor had served as surgeon in the army during the war, and was a man of excellent acquirements and quick perceptions.

"I have seen you before, I think, at Mrs. Winchester's, Mr. Dale?" he said carelessly, when the bandage had fallen short, and Mrs. Owen had hurried away with thumping footsteps for more old cotton. "It was when a little grandson of hers had a bad fall in the stable," he explained, holding the strip of cloth with firm fingers.

"Yes," replied Dick Dale uneasily. "I thought I had seen you. If you run across any of my people, don't speak of my being here. I stopped to make a sketch or two, and meant to be away to-day. I have promised to visit my aunt later in the season," he added more boldly. He was unaccustomed to apologizing for his plans, and wondered, as he spoke, why he felt now a little at odds with propriety.

The doctor nodded, and seemed indisposed to criticise the deeds of any young man, especially an artist. "You could not find a more picturesque bit of country," he said, with considerable enthusiasm. "There were two or three artists staying at the east village in June. I dare say they might have been friends of yours."

Mrs. Owen had returned with a stout roll of linen and a damaged sheet, which she offered submissively for inspection. "There's plenty more where this come from," she announced, a little out of breath; and the doctor smilingly responded that she had better not let any of the hospitals hear of her; they were always beggared for want of such things.

"Will he be laid up a good while, do you suppose?" she asked the hurried surgeon, with a shade of anxiety, as she followed him to the door, and hardly knew whether she was most relieved or disappointed when the doctor answered that this sprain was only slight; it was a miserable weak ankle; the fellow had used it too soon after the first injury.

The morning went by slowly, and Dale grew more and more dissatisfied and impatient with himself. He had heard the doctor's verdict upon his case, and did not anticipate any long delay; but his foot ached badly, and the bandage felt tight and bungling, though it looked so smooth and irreproachable. He had been established in a high-backed wooden rocking-chair in the clock-room, with his lame foot on another chair, cushioned by a small and fluffy pillow, with a cover so long that it drooped to the floor and looked like a baby's skimpy-frock. He was left to himself for a time. Doris was going to Dunster without him, and would bring back Temperance Kipp, the maid servant, and his own portmanteau. Dale could see her in the yard harnessing a horse into a light wagon. Presently her mother joined her, looking heated from her work in the kitchen. She was a fine, straight woman for her years, a most kind creature, the young man thought gratefully, and smiled as he heard her tell Doris what the doctor had said, and add that the disabled foot was as soft and white as a child's. Doris seemed impatient to be off. The young horse she drove was impatient, also, and whirled the wagon round a corner of the yard and down the road. Dale leaned forward to see better. Doris looked quickly up at the window, and their eyes exactly met; the next moment she was hidden by the willow boughs, but it was so still about the farm that the sound of wheels could be heard for some minutes.

Mrs. Owen looked in, every little while, and always said that they were going to have a regular dog-day. The tall clock ticked excitedly, as if it were not pleased with this intrusion upon its own apartment. The county paper lay upon the table under the looking-glass, with the Massachusetts Ploughman and the semi-weekly Tribune, which Dale selected with satisfaction. After looking over its pages with sad quickness, he made use of it to beat away the flies which were flocking in from the kitchen. Mrs. Owen had unguardedly left the door half open, and they seemed eager to prove the truth of her repeated statement about the weather. From his seat by the window he could see the hillside and the orchard, with the small, pathetic crowd of gray and white headstones in the family burying-place. One might fancy that these stones were a sort of prosaic disguise, under which the former dwellers in the old farmhouse stood apart together to watch and comment gloomily upon their descendants. The faded little flag alone signified any active interest. There was a kind of hopeful beckoning and inspiration about its slight movements and flutterings.

In the dullest of the morning hours Dick was assured that he must communicate with his aunt, and make use of her hospitality. Later, he reflected that, however reasonable such an arrangement might appear, it would be also a great bore. The house was always well filled at this time of the summer. There was sure to be a flock of his aunt's grandchildren, and they were noisy and clamorous enough if a man were well, and he was not disposed to put himself at their mercy now, confounded little beggars! They were all extremely fond of him, and hitherto he had returned their affection with a more or less spasmodic warmth. Dick jerked his shoulders suddenly, as if a first-cousin, once removed, had unsympathetically tried to climb upon them. He would wait a day or two, and see how the ankle got on; indeed, he had often spent a week or two in a duller place than this. But he wondered idly, more than once, if it were not time for Doris to be at home again.

VII.

MEANWHILE work was going forward on the marshes. There had been some delay in transporting the crew of men; the great hay-boat, which had not been used before for some months, was stranded high and dry on the shore at the side of the creek. It had been well beached, and put as far out of reach of the spring tides as possible, lest it should float off across the shallow sea which covered the meadows, and be either wrecked or take up its residence inconveniently far inland. The same spring tide, however, had revenged itself for the loss of its prey by giving the heavy boat a lift and a push which made it swing about and tug at its moorings from the opposite direction. Finally, when the waters receded from their unnatural vantage ground, the craft settled down heavily, with its bow toward the deep channel; and when the huckleberry and bayberry bushes waked up a little later, they struggled and bent their twigs under a weight and obscurity equal to a land-slide, and concluded that it was not spring yet, after all.

The farmer had met such hindrances before, and had laid some persuasive rollers in the way to the water, and the launch was achieved in the early August morning with little difficulty, though with the aid of much shouting at the horses from Jim Fales, beside vigorous pushing from all the haymakers. The tide was in, and the stupid-looking square hay-boat floated lightly, with a somewhat coquettish air of being in its element, while the displaced water splashed among the coarse grass of the shore. A weather-beaten dory was brought up and fastened at the hay-boat's stern; the farmer was carefully putting his scythes and pitchforks on board. One of the men fastened the horses to a small maple-tree, which they browsed industriously. Doris was to come presently to drive them back to the barn.

Jim Fales had worked furiously to aid the launching of the hay-boat, and now stood contemplating it with some scorn. "Ain't she got a sassy bow?" he remarked derisively. "I don't know 's I ever see one that was built more awk'ard. 'T was one o' old Lester's make, wa'n't it? His was all the same pattern."

"You take right holt now, my son, and help git these tools aboard," said Israel Owen serenely. "We're belated more'n I wish we was a'ready. An' Lester's bo'ts are pretty much all afloat in the ma'shes now, while those that have been made since are mostly split or rotten. He put good stuff into 'em, and they carry well, a good load and well set, if they be square-nosed."

"We'll all be drownded, sure's fate. I guess I'd better step along on the bank," laughed the young man; "she's leakin' like a sieve."

"Give her a couple of hours in the water and she'll be as dry as a cup," said the farmer. "I know her. But run along ashore if you feel skeary, James," as the youngster leaped lightly over the side. The other men smiled indulgently. Jim Fales was a good fellow, whose faults were those of youth and self-confidence. He was thin and light, quick as a flash, and apt to work beyond his strength in boyish bravado. He was employed at men's wages for the first time this summer, and had proved himself worthy to enter the lists at any sort of farm-work, though some of his comrades could not help wondering how he would hold out. He was frequently designated as the Grasshopper, and was worth at least half his pay for his good spirits and the amusement he afforded his associates.

One would have thought that the boat's builder had measured the width of the creek before he laid her timbers, and then left very little room on either side. The complication which would be involved by one hay-boat's meeting another in the deep and narrow channels of the marsh can hardly be pictured, unless, indeed, the crews were amicably transferred. At some distance, however, a broader inlet was shining in the morning sunlight, and another boat and its company presently emerged from behind a point of the Marsh Island, and floated placidly away to the eastward.

"There goes Bennet's folks," said Mr. Jenks. "They're late this morning, too," and Jim Fales and Allen, who were poling, doubled their diligence, and made haste to signify their presence by loud and echoing outcries.

Farmer Owen had seated himself on the broad gunwale of his valued boat, leaning forward, with his elbows on his knees and his brown hands clasped together before him.

Sometimes the tall sedges brushed the faded cambric back of his waistcoat, and once Mr. Jenks reached out and cut two or three cattails with his great jack-knife, and selecting the largest proceeded to trim it, and then stuck it in a small auger hole in the stern, where it looked like the mockery of a mast. For some distance the faded square of yellow was visible where the boat had lain on the sloping bank; it made a surprisingly attractive point in the landscape, and Farmer Owen said once, as he looked at it, that the growth underneath would be likely to think there was an early fall. There had been no such high tides for ten years as the spring before, when Lester's masterpiece had been drifted so far ashore.

As they neared a point half-way to the south marsh, a young man was seen standing there, waiting, a solitary figure on the low shore. This was Dan Lester, who, as the hay-boat approached, took a flying leap and landed in what might be called the hold, making a great splash in the six or seven inches of water, which seemed to disconcert neither him nor anybody else.

"I'd better have fetched a mallet and

spike along, and caulked up this conveyance," he said soberly, with an inward sense of the scrutiny of Jim Fales's curious eyes. His mind was not at ease, and he tried to behave exactly as usual, without entire success.

"I guess 't will be the end o' the leakage now," Israel Owen announced, after a wondering though brief look at this new member of the crew. "The sides are tight, and 't was only the bottom planks that had shrunk a grain, same 's they do every year. She 'll be dry enough if she lays out in this sun till evenin'."

The fresh morning wind ruffled the surface of the tide river and tossed about the foliage on the shore, lifting the leaves and varying their shades of green skillfully. As the boat slowly rounded a point covered with underbrush, Lester saw a late wild rose almost within reach of his hand, and with the sudden thought of Doris that was always linked in his mind with anything beautiful he tried to catch and break the twig. But he had been carried just too far beyond, and almost fell over into the water. The other men laughed, and he joined them a little ruefully, and watched the flower, as if the loss of it foretold his fate. He had known the misery and anxiety of an unassured lover the night before. He had never until now been really uncertain or in such desperate earnest about winning Doris, and was shaken and hurt by his sleeplessness and fears. Dan was a model of health and vigor. Like men of his nature, he could ill bear suffering of any sort, but he was supported this morning by a noble instinct of heroism. He would die hard before he let himself betray the lack of courage that he sometimes felt. If Doris knew how troubled he was for her sake, she could not help thinking that he deserved her love. Poor fellow! sometimes he needed her tender pity almost as much.

But saucy Jim Fales, with his quick, shrewd eyes, had dared to tell him that he looked afflicted, and was begging him to give the reason. It was a preposterous favor to ask, under the circumstances, and Jim seemed quite abominable. Lester was quick-tempered, and found himself growing very angry, although it would never do to wage open war against the youngster. Mr. Owen was already looking benignly at the faces of his companions, as if he were becoming conscious of the presence of some interest he did not understand.

They were so far away now from the farm that it showed its whole outline and extent from that eastern point of view. The hill which Dick Dale thought a good lookout had lowered itself, and was only a bare, unsheltered pasture upland. Israel Owen could read at a glance all the slopes and hollows of the woodland and fields of the neighboring country, and surveyed with pleasure his own sound fences and the tops of his fruit-trees, which showed themselves over the crest of the island as if they were trying to see what was on the seaward side.

The tide was full; the lines of the creeks made a broad tracery whichever way one looked. Northward and southward from the Marsh Island the great reaches of the Sussex marshes spread themselves level and green, while the nearer hills of the inland country were bronzed and autumn-like, and the distant ones were blue in the morning haze. The sea-birds overhead were crying and calling, as if they besought the salt-hay makers to fly away with them, like reluctant nestlings of their own.

The outlying portion of Israel Owen's property, toward which he was voyaging, was a low bit of the sea country. Even this not unusual tide was submerging its borders, and most of the grass must be taken away to be spread and dried elsewhere. The old farmer with Dan Lester went apart from the other workmen, and all began to mow as fast as possible, so that a good portion of the crop might be put into the boat, ready to carry away when the tide should be high again in the evening. The men stepped forward diligently; the tall grasses fell before their enemies, rank after rank. The tide held itself bravely for a time: it had grasped the land nobly; all that great weight and power were come in and had prevailed. It shone up at the sky; and laughed in the sun's face; then changed its mind, and began to creep away again. It would rise no more that morning, but at night the world should wonder! So the great sea, forsaking its purpose, slid back out of the narrow creeks and ditches, leaving them black and deep, with the green sedge drooping over their edges; and at midday the sun was fierce and hot, and the haymakers brought the small sail of the dory, and made a tent-like shelter of it with their pitchforks, and were ready for their nooning.

"I declare I don't know 's it was ever hotter than this any of the hot days I've seen in my time," said the farmer. "Doris had a notion yisterday that 't would be better for her to bring over the dinner at noontime; she thought she could slip down the west crick in her small bo't, if 't was low water; but I'm glad she didn't." The younger men gave each other a sly look; they would have enjoyed such a visit in the midst of their dull work. Some evil spirit suggested to Jim Fales that it would be good fun to tease Dan Lester.

"Doris!" he exclaimed contemptuously. "She'll be all taken up with the city swell, I expect; she won't have no time to spare for country folks. Perhaps she'll fetch him along over here in her dory, long towards night when it gits cooler, to make a picture of us."

"He looks like my boy Isr'el," said Farmer Owen, unexpectedly. "She's going to take him in to Dunster to git his trunk, — Doris is. Mis' Owen, she's calc'latin' to accommodate him for a spell." And one of the haymakers, who had been hungry enough the moment before, put down what would have been his next mouthful as if the bread were a stone. Jim Fales whistled at the sight, and the lover shot a fierce glance at him. What a fool he was making of himself, he thought piteously, the next minute, and tried to go on with his lunch. Mrs. Owen was a capital cook and provider, but Lester wondered how he could dispose of his share, while young Fales ventured to say satirically that he thought he had seen a snake; and being wonderingly answered by the proprietor that they were never common on the south marsh, held his peace.

Some of the men stretched themselves out for a nap, and Dan Lester feigned to copy their example; but when he left his hard couch, a little later, to join his employer, it was with sullen, tired eyes, and a determination to ask Doris's father a solemn question.

Farmer Owen had apparently taken no notice of Jim Fales's ostentatious discovery of the reptile, nor of the personal character of the talk, but Dan Lester looked dark, and muttered as if he were a strayed thunder-cloud. A light breeze had risen, and the stillness of the unusual heat was over with, but the young man grew flushed and warm, and stood holding his scythe as if it were an aggressive weapon, while he fanned himself with his frayed straw hat. He was a handsome fellow, dark and thin and straight, with a suggestion of French blood in his remote ancestry. A pair of honest blue eyes looked unrelated to his brown cheeks, and an inch or less above them there was a sharp dividing line between his singularly white forehead and the dusky tints below. The old farmer glanced toward him once or twice compassionately, and at last came and laid a heavy hand kindly upon Dan's shoulder.

"Don't cry before ye're hurt, lad," he said. "Don't take no account of that youngster's nonsense, neither; 't ain't wuth your while, as I view it."

Lester flushed again, and looked more angry than before; his first impulse was to accuse his annoyers and defend himself, but luckily he became aware of the opportunity to plead his cause with Doris's father. He choked down his silly wrath, and a gentle, almost pleading expression came into his face; no words could be found for a minute, and the elder man stood waiting patiently. "Come," he said at last, "we must get to work."

"I've been wanting to speak with you," Lester whispered, as if they might be overheard even at that distance from their companions. "I do set everything by Doris. I feel as if I wanted to make certain I had a right to her."

"I can't say but I'm willin'," answered the farmer. "I should like to see it come about, far's I'm concerned. Have ye spoke with her last night, may be?" and he looked hopefully at his would-be son-in-law's transparent countenance. "Your father and me, we was always the best of friends. I'd rather have you master of the old place than anybody about, so long's poor Isr'el never 'll want it."

"I tried to screw me up to say something or 'nother, so she'd know, as we was ridin' along last evenin'," said Dan, grateful for the listener's confidence. "I don't know 's I'm chicken-hearted, but I could n't speak my mind. Seems if she must know, too. I wish the women was the ones that spoke first, they'd get over it a sight the easiest;" and Dan tried to laugh, but his mirth was not sincere. "She's too good for me by a long shot, but I never 'll let her want for nothin', specially lovin' kindness," he burst out, with such excitement that the next moment a reaction followed his unwonted sentiment, and he felt afraid that his old friend would laugh at him.

"Yes, yes!" the elder man exclaimed somewhat impatiently. "I don't feel uneasy, Dan, an' 't will all come right in time. She ain't sure of her own mind p'rhaps, but 't is set that way. Women 's a kind of game: you 've got to hunt 'em their own track, an' when you 've caught 'em they 've got to be tamed some. Strange, ain't it? — they most all on 'em calc'late to git married; and yet it goes sort of against their natur', too, and seems hard to come to, for the most part:" and Mr. Owen shook his head solemnly over this difficult question, and walked away slowly to his work. Lester's mind felt not wholly unburdened, but this was at least a good beginning. "The old gentleman don't make so clean a cut this year as I 've seen him," he thought. "I 'll borrow some excuse to get him to quit work early;" and then Dan gave his own scythe a vigorous whetting, and mowed with surprising effect all the afternoon. Perhaps the stranger at the farmhouse was gone already. No, the farmer had said that his wife was going to take him to board for some days; and Dan felt an unusual sense of bitterness toward the good woman who seemed to be so unfriendly to his cause. Perhaps the painter was a married man. It was no use to be distressed, and Doris had been very good-humored the evening before, as they drove to the choir-meeting. Yet as the hours went by he grew more and more anxious to see her again.

As for Jim Fales and Mr. Jenks and Allen, they were filled with vain imaginings, and made themselves particularly merry over the lover's exasperation. "Land, how we'll thorn Dan up to-morrow telling how him and her was keeping company in the best room, and walking up in the orchard after dark!" said Jim Fales. "There, now; see the old sir a' clappin' him on the shoulder! He's going to say, Bless you, my child'n, sure's you're alive."

"He seemed mightily taken with the city chap, it struck me," said Mr. Jenks, who had worked in one of the Sussex shipyards all summer, and had lately been thrown out of employment by the dull season. "And look here, young man, you'd best keep out o' the range of Dan Lester's fist, if you've set your mind on baiting him." Mr. Jenks was a man of few words, and his junior looked disappointed and grave at this unexpected warning.

"I don' know 's we 've got to settle everything for 'em this afternoon; but Dan's well stirred up and jealous as sin, ain't he?" inquired Jim, a few minutes afterward, in a serious tone. "I should n't wonder myself if it set him on to get matters fixed to his mind. He 's been goin' with Doris Owen ever since I can remember. He was a big boy to school when I was a little one in the primer."

"He come from about here, did n't he?" asked Allen, who was a stranger in the neighborhood, though known to Mr. Jenks by means of the shipyards and other commercial interests.

"Right over beyond the cross-roads," answered Fales, "where the crick makes in. His father and grandfather was the best bo't-builders anywhere about; but Dan's father, he died young, and his mother married again to old Lawton, and a mighty poor business 't was," said the young philosopher sagely. "She 'd done a sight better to stop where she was. Dan was always warrin' with the old man, and nobody blamed him.

Dan had a good property from his father's folks, and his mother did n't know enough to hold on to it, and about all of it leaked away. You never see anybody step cheerfuller than Dan did to the burying-ground, when the old fellow was gathered. He was squiring his mother at the head o' the procession, sleevin' of her handsome, as if he liked it. Dan 's well off: he 's been an awful lucky fellow, and some of his money that grandsir Lawton did n't borrow turned out first-rate. I should n't be surprised if he was worth pretty near five thousand dollars to-day."

"That won't go 's fur as it used to, in maintainin' a wife," said Jenks. His generous lunch seemed to have put him in a talkative temper. "Five thousand dollars used to be called a smart property, but nowadays folks has to have so many notions; everybody must stick a couple o' bay winders out front of their houses, else they ain't considered Christian. Bill Simms had to do it, for all his place was stuck as full o' lights as a lantern a'ready. I guess he finds he 's got took in with his new companion. There was plenty warned him, but he would n't hear to reason; he 'd been told she 'd got means."

"She's a homely creatur' enough," spoke Allen eagerly. "I see her out loppin' over the fence middle o' the morning, day before yisterday. Where 'd she come from, anyway? Where 'd Simms pick her up?"

"I b'lieve 't was over Seabrook way," drawled Mr. Jenks, stooping to take wider reaches at the grass. "I d' know whether she was drove ashore or whether he took her on a trawl, I 'm sure, sir;" and this unusual turn of Mr. Jenks's conversation forced his comrades to laugh heartily. Indeed, the sound of their merriment beguiled Israel Owen from his thoughts of the past and Dan Lester from his hopes of the future, and they laughed back again with instinctive sympathy.

VIII.

THAT afternoon Mr. Dale made himself delightfully agreeable. Mrs. Owen felt more than equal to the situation, and had already welcomed back the burly strength and reassuring cheerfulness of Temperance Kipp. This excellent person had grown up, or been raised, as she would have expressed it, on the farm, and remained loyal now to her early friends, in spite of the enticements of well-to-do members of her own family.

Dick rejoiced in his recovered personal belongings, which Temperance herself brought in from the wagon and placed beside him, urged to this service by an insatiable curiosity to see the guest of whom Doris had spoken. Her opinion was extremely favorable, and after a short time the good woman came downstairs quite shorn of her holiday garb, and resumed her duties in the household. Dick remembered a frequent expression of Mrs. Owen's as he caught an occasional glimpse of Temperance; he could well believe that she was always to be depended upon, yet he had an instant sense that she was not likely to take his part. Indeed one may think himself lucky whose enemies do not rank themselves in overpowering numbers, for woe be to the man whose nature is instinctively at war with others. Dick was so well used to finding himself in harmonious relations with his associates that he was for the moment shocked when Temperance's shrewd eyes regarded him with suspicion, and he at once determined to make friends with her.

By and by, after the early dinner was disposed of, Doris came with her sewing, to sit on the shaded step of the side door, outside the clock-room. The two elder women also kept the sufferer company. He told some capital stories, and spoke with exceeding wisdom and sympathy of certain aspects of farm life; he also praised his surroundings with rare discretion. Mrs. Owen was immensely pleased with Dick. She had an air of being even proud of him, and assured him in a most motherly way that he could give no trouble, and must take his own time about the pictures, and make himself at home.

But the day seemed a week long to both Doris and the painter. As for Dick Dale, he wondered, in the course of his afternoon's entertainment, if he might not be growing gray. He was used to a social aspect of life and to good-fellowship, but they were enjoying each other that day in the clock-room until it was fairly suffocating. Yet when Doris appeared in her cool afternoon dress, slender and shy and silent, his first pleasure returned. The salt breeze that came in from the sea as the sun grew low sent a delicious freshness through the house, and Dale looked out of the window, and wondered why he had not liked the view so much before. He spoke to Doris with gentle deference, quite unlike his frank comradeship with the other women; and she blushed a little as she answered his questions, and then blushed again to think she had blushed at all. Dale could see her from his chair, which was kept from rocking with extreme difficulty. He presently took from his pocket a book which he had chosen when he first opened his portmanteau. The not very orderly but familiar contents of that receptacle had given him a curious feeling of exile with an assurance of comfort, and as he made an evident signal of discontinuance to the conversation, Temperance and her mistress rose and went their ways. Dick would have liked to try reading aloud, but he was not prepared to take the risk of a great disappointment. Doris certainly looked as if she would know the meaning of such true poetry, and he glanced at his young hostess from time to time, and wished that it were possible to stroll through the upper orchard again, with her for company.

When the sun was low Doris came to look at the industrious old time-keeper, and then hurried away up the yard to the barns. Dick wistfully heard the horses stamp and her emphatic commands, and he listened with eager interest, a few minutes later, to a sound of wheels receding, and muffled by the soft grass. Doris must be going down to the creek again to meet the haymakers. Was it her father whom she wished to serve, or the lover, who was also at work on the marshes?

Doris herself was filled with a strange excitement that day. She was finding her own thoughts and actions painfully unfamiliar, and felt as if she were looking at them through another person's eyes. When she reached the landing-place she could not have explained why the bleached grass and twigs, which the hay-boat had kept from light and growth all summer, struck a respondent chord in her own mind. It might be that a weight of inapprehension and necessity of routine was lifted from her consciousness; but whether the coming of the young stranger had hastened this, or only marked it, no one could know. Doris became more and more disturbed; her thoughts busied themselves provokingly with Dan Lester and that fear of danger and impending crisis which had troubled her the evening before. She was not ready to listen to what she was certain Dan wished to say; her anticipation of the future reached no farther yet than her lover's proposal, and by no means made clear her own answer. Presently Doris was reminded of the morning's accident. The stranger's helplessness and pain had roused all her womanly pity and eagerness to be of use, yet something had taken away her power of action, and forbade such traits to show themselves. Her mother had never made her so impatient before. The homely expressions of concern and excitement seemed quite needless; but Mrs. Owen was ready with prompt service and simple remedies, while Doris herself only grew more self-conscious and distressed.

She hated her own silliness, and thought of many things now as she stood waiting at the landing; but the twilight fell before the tired and hungry haymakers made their appearance. Once or twice she climbed the hill a little way, to watch for the dory. The silence of the place was very soothing, and she liked to hear the notes of birds, piping clear and untroubled from a thicket not far away. There were two thrushes answering each other with sweetest voices from tree to tree, and Doris leaned against the horse's warm shoulder and listened contentedly. She was glad that it would not do to leave the horse alone: it is a curious dislike that such domesticated creatures have to being left to themselves in lonely places. At last the sound of voices and of dipping oars came drifting through the still air, and the girl waited eagerly for her father's greeting.

It came presently, cheerful and pleased, and Doris answered. Then she saw that there was an unexpected person in the boat, five men in all, and hardly knew why she wished for some reprieve or defense, and even grew rigidly silent with displeasure. A minute later Dan Lester leaped ashore. "You and me'll walk up to the house, Doris," he said, decidedly. "It's a pretty evening." The other workmen were hurriedly landing their tools; they had not observed Dan's words, as Doris had angrily supposed. "I shall have to ride with father," she answered, coldly. "I must go right home now to help about supper."

This was very unlike her usual quiet friendliness. The young man stood still for a moment, looking at her; then, as she turned, he said, "Good-night, all!" and also turned away, crashing through the bushes as if he meant to take the straightest way toward his own home. Israel Owen looked after him wonderingly.

"I wish you would stop to supper, Dan!" he shouted, a moment afterward, but presently mounted the long wagon. Jim Fales sat in the end of it, swinging his feet, but the other men tramped alongside. The flash of unreasonable anger faded from the girl's mind. She was sorry that she had hurt Dan's feelings, — he was always so friendly; but she had not liked his speaking so before the rest. . . . The sky was clear and the air was very soft; there were only a few fragments of bluish cloud against the narrow band of rose color in the west. Doris could not help thinking that a walk over the hill and down through the orchard might have been pleasant, after all.

Dan Lester heard the farmer's anxious inquiry about some accident that had happened, and presently somebody spoke of the doctor. He was not far away, poor Dan; the thick hedgerow of black cherry-trees and underbrush prevented anybody's seeing him at the other side of a stone wall. "Dear! dear!" said Mr. Owen anxiously, once or twice; and the lover was sorry he had been so impatient, and would have given anything to know what had happened at the farmhouse. Perhaps he would walk up after dark; they might not have been able to bring Temperance back from Dunster, — and Dan hurried homeward along a faint trail of a footpath which crossed the dewy fields and a wide pasture. He blamed himself more and more for not going to the Owens' at once, but there was certainly something strange in Doris's behavior. He did not often make such a fool of himself as he had that night. If Doris's mother were ill, she would have told her father at once, or have sought him earlier. Perhaps the painter had met with an accident, and Dan concluded to have a look at him before an hour later. This kindly fellow was suddenly transformed into a vindictive, suspicious enemy of any person who could thwart his long-cherished love. Twenty-four hours were indeed a short time for a stranger to have gained much vantage-ground, but after all Doris Owen was a woman.

Dick Dale thought the men amusingly curious and excited about his slight accident. By this time it was quite an old story to everybody else. Each haymaker professed to have met with exactly the same disaster, and to be acquainted with the only infallible remedy. As for Doris, her expression had changed surprisingly; she looked hurt and impatient, and when she brought a tray with Dick's supper, she cast an appealing look into his very eyes. He became sure that something troubled her, and gave her more than one compassionate glance in return.

IX.

WESTWARD from the farm, beyond an expanse of almost level country, a low range of hills made a near horizon. They were gray in the drought, and bare like a piece of moorland, save where the fences barred them, or a stunted tree stood up against the sky, leaning away from the winter storms toward a more sheltered and fertile inland region. The windward side of the Marsh Island itself was swept clean by the sea winds; it was only on the southern and western slopes that the farmer's crops, his fruit-trees, and his well-stocked garden found encouragement to grow. Eastward, on the bleak downs, a great flock of sheep nibbled and strayed about all day, and blinked their eyes at the sun. The island was a thrifty estate; going backward a little in these latest years, the neighbors whispered, but more like an old-country habitation than many homes of this newer world.

The salt-hay making was over at last. The

marshes were dotted as far as eye could see by the round haystacks with their deftly pointed tops. These gave a great brilliance of color to the landscape, being unfaded yet by the rain and snow that would dull their yellow tints later in the year. September weather came early, even before its appointed season, and there was a constant suggestion of autumn before the summer was fairly spent. The delicate fragrance of the everlasting-flowers was plainly noticeable in the dry days that followed each other steadily. The summer was ripe early this year, and the fruits reddened, and the flowers all went to seed, and the days grew shorter in kindly fashion, being so pleasant that one could not resent the hurrying twilight, or now and then the acknowledged loss of a few minutes of daylight. From the top of the island hill a great fading countryside spread itself wide and fair, and seaward the sails looked strangely white against the deepened blue of the ocean. There were more coasting-vessels than could usually be seen, even in midsummer, as if great flocks of them had grown that year, like the birds.

In these days, nobody stopped to think much about Dick Dale's lingering at the farmhouse. His temporary invalidism was the cause of most friendly relations with all the family; his presence appeared completely natural and inevitable. When he had given Israel Owen an excellent drawing made from the small picture of the soldier, there was no longer any question of the artist's being welcome to anything upon the island. Dick had taken great pains with this experiment in portrait-making. He told himself that he was not ashamed of it, either, though he was most grateful for having had some aid to contentment during the few days he had kept his lamed foot still in the clock-room. He was not without his fancies about the portrait's subject; for as he worked he had a vague consciousness of an unseen presence, and some most telling touches were made almost in spite of himself. He thought often of the possible unseen dwellers in such old houses, and as he resumed his out-of-door rambles it was with a continued sense of companionship, or as if another were sharing the use of his own eyes.

Though the mistress of the house had often spoken scornfully of those who sold their peace of mind and parted with all sovereignty and comfort in their homes to rapacious summer boarders, the presence of this quiet and courteous young gentleman in her own household appeared quite another thing. He did not make the daily work seem any more burdensome; on the contrary, he gave a pleasant flavor of holiday-making to her life. Everybody liked to please Dick, and, to do him justice, he tried not infrequently to give pleasure as well as take it; he knew how to confer a favor by the way he received one. To him the situation grew more and more satisfactory and almost ideal. There was a patriarchal character to the family. The gentle old farmer, with his flocks and herds and his love for his lands, was a charming example of the repose and peace to be gained from country life; it all contrasted strangely with the mode of existence Dale had known best. Sometimes he shut his eyes and tried to fancy the familiar racket outside his city windows. The English sparrows in their one smoke-blackened tree had alone reminded him that there was such life as this in the world. He assured himself again and again that he must send for Bradish, his studio partner and best crony, to come and share these treasures; but day after day went by, and still Dick delayed to write. He thought with scorn of those acquaintances who believed themselves bound to walk and drive and dine and sleep only at fashionable hours. They might read the same books, if they chose, and praise the same things as completely as the usual diversifications of human nature would allow. There was nothing so satisfactory as to step ashore out of the great current, — " Things are of the snake," quoted our hero, and was thankful for once that he was busy just at the time when so large a part of the world is idle. Since his student days in France he had done the lightest possible work at his profession, but now he was fired by an ambition to carry back to town some sufficient evidence of his skill and perception. Bradish and other comrades of his own were hard-working fellows, who found the American public absurdly economical in respect to art. They despised entirely that bad taste which allows a householder to pay five hundred dollars for a carpet, without annoyance, and to shrink from the extravagance of giving the tenth of that amount for a good sketch. Bradish, for whom our hero had a sincere friendship, was a generous young man, whose purse was usually empty; and it must be confessed that Dale quietly paid a large proportion of the studio bills, more for his comrade's sake than his own. But he must give the little group of painters some reason for their fond belief that he could do better things than any of them, if he tried; and it might be as well to reëstablish his claim to belong to a circle of workers instead of drifting on as a well-known figure in general society.

Besides, there was a pleasing sense of having hidden away from the curious world, and it was wise to enjoy this while it lasted. Dale was much amused at watching the effect upon himself of being transplanted by a whimsical fate into that rural neighborhood. He was well endowed with practical gifts, though one must acknowledge that these were combined in an apparently unpractical character, and a few alterations and rearrangements in the rooms of the farmhouse made it much more interesting than it had ever been before. He liked it too well as it was to suggest many actual changes, but he rescued more than one piece of old Delft or mahogany from ignoble uses, and deeply enjoyed and profited by Mrs. Owen's generous exhibition of her household furnishings. She professed a vast indifference to his most cherished discoveries; it was the farmer whose sentiment and discernment were delicate enough to follow Dick far in his æsthetic enthusiasms. Doris, who watched and wondered, and moved about the old house with gentle quickness, enjoyed this new dispensation more than anybody else. She was made like her father. Some of their ancestors had been of gentle blood and high consideration in the old days of the colonies; her home-loving womanly pride bloomed now in new freedom and delight. What Mrs. Owen had in former years contemptuously spoken of as Doris's notions were referred to and paraded with motherly satisfaction. Sometimes the girl's heart was filled with confusion, because her mother, in some cordial, garrulous moment, unveiled one of the lesser shrines of her own nature. There was a sacred reserve in Doris: her inmost heart could not put itself into speech; she was only frightened and grieved when another dared to be noisy in her sweet silences. As for her own talk, it was apt to be so childishly simple, that those who wished to know her feelings must watch her eyes. With all her shyness, she had a way of forcing one to meet her eyes fully, and the tale they told was remembered afterward, while the words of her lips were forgotten.

There was a studio now on the Marsh Island, — a place wholly picturesque and delightful to its occupant. Dick had early discovered an upper room, with an outer stairway, over the narrow chaise-house, and was told that the women of the family had once gone there in summer weather to do their spinning. In such coolness and airiness, at the edge of the orchard, there must have been almost a festival, as the wool-wheels and flax-wheels whirred and merry voices chattered together. There had formerly been a loom, also, but it had been taken to pieces; and when Dale first explored the spinning-room it was quite empty except for some damaged ears of seed-corn which the rats had rolled about the floor. The artist inspected these quarters eagerly. He looked out of a square north window at the apple-trees and a glimpse of blue water. Opposite he saw the back of the old farm-house, with its quaint joiner-work half hidden by a woodbine flecked with red; beyond that, past the great willows, was the barren range of hills, already purple in the afternoon light. It was impossible not to return to the family at once with the suggestion of such possible ease and comfort in artistic pursuit. By that time next day, with the aid of some sober-tinted rugs which Temperance deemed the worst of her manufacture, and some ancient chairs that had hardly been thought fit even for a place in the kitchen; with a claw-footed table and a tall cider mug to hold a handful of flowers, the spinning-room delighted even Mrs. Owen. She laughed good-naturedly at the promotion of her disdained possessions, but the fanciful wayfarer stood proudly in the doorway to take a last look, while the good people went away. It was supper-time, and he was not disposed to be late, but he assured himself that such a studio would really make Bradish howl.

There was plenty of material for sketches to be had without straying far, and for some time Dick thought little of anything but his pictures. It was a busy month at the farm, with the successive harvestings; but he learned to greatly enjoy and to depend not a little upon the interest and comments of his housemates. As he leaned back in his chair, late one afternoon, to take a somewhat disheartening view of his work, he scarcely noticed at first that some one stood in the doorway. The sun was low, and filled the little room with golden light. The unfinished picture should have looked its best with such a halo, but Dale pushed back the easel with dangerous roughness, and gathered his brushes with an impatient hand. "Ah, Doris, is that you?" he said, more coldly than usual, and Doris smiled in unnecessary assent.

She did not often appear so interested and so comfortably forgetful of herself as that day. She stepped inside the room, and her face glowed with pleasure at the artist's unfinished work. "I like that better than anything you have painted, Mr. Dale," she said simply; and then, as if nobody need say anything else, she waited quietly, looking at the canvas with evident delight. It seemed as if she had a sudden revelation of the pleasantness of the little room and its contents, or rather as if she had been pleased already by something that had happened before she came to the spinning-room.

"I am very glad," Dale answered, beginning to take heart again. "I tore up one of the best water-colors I ever made, because I was too tired to like it when it was done."

"Oh, what a pity!" Doris whispered softly.

They had grown to be very good friends, though the girl was often elusive, and placed some indefinable barrier about herself. He was not the only person who felt its presence. Dale thought sometimes that Nature had made a mistake in putting this soul into so tall and commanding a body; perhaps Doris would have been more at ease in the world if she had been smaller; the sort of woman whom everybody takes care of and pets, if they have a right. But Nature could work out her own wise plans, and this fine, strong character would be ready to answer great demands as well as little ones. Martha Owen announced in these days that it had done Doris good to have Mr. Dale stay at the farm, — it had waked her up a little; but she would always be just like her father!

Doris was looking her very best, this September afternoon, in a simple white dress which had once been worn only on the finest and hottest summer Sundays. She had taken it for every-day use this year. To-day she had picked up a small broken twig of cider apples which had fallen from one of the old trees, and put it in her belt. The green leaves and the paler tints of the clustered dwarfed fruit, heightened here and there with a dash of red, were most charming, and Dale looked at Doris with great pleasure while she looked at the picture.

Presently she roused herself from her short reverie with a little sigh: "Oh, I came to ask you if you could find it convenient to go to Sussex with me to-morrow morning. Mother wants to send, and we remembered that you spoke about going, a while ago," and Doris looked in his face with childish eagerness. "Mother and Temp'rance and I have been as busy as bees all this week. I don't like to be drudging in-doors, this splendid weather," she added, with a rare little laugh. Dale was always delighted when she laughed; she was more apt to smile slowly and gravely, like her father.

Doris's plea of drudgery was almost unfounded; she was apparently less fettered by duty than the rest of the family, and this would not be the first drive they had taken. Mrs. Owen was only too willing for the young people to be together, and the farmer never objected. Yet Dick had become less familiar with them all rather than more, since he had involved himself in his work, and his first delight at his surroundings had ripened into more practical acquaintance. Latterly they had followed their own pursuits, and taken little heed of each other's. As for Dan Lester, he seemed to have disappeared altogether. The evening of Dick's accident was the last time he had come to the house. Dick himself suspected that there had been some quarrel; but to-night, at any rate, Doris was sufficiently lighthearted. Within a few days she had individualized herself in a strange way; he thought of her a great deal more than usual, and felt a new interest in her works and ways. So marked a growth of sympathy there was that he told himself she had been only a part of the general attractiveness of the Marsh Island at first. He had always liked to watch her, and had enjoyed her charming outlines and her coloring, in the same way that he made the most of the looks and behavior of one of the old willows. Doris was a woman, and the willow was a tree; but that had not made any difference in his feeling except one of degree. He began to wonder what her future would be, and gave a quick shrug at its probable inadequacy to her capabilities. He was curious to see Lester again, though quite thankful to him for taking himself off. Dick had been conscious of an instinctive liking for his rival when he had first entered the clockroom, divining the truth that the poor fellow was showing his worst side, either from some awkwardness or fancied injury and opposition.

The farmer had spoken a few grateful words in recognition of Lester's generous service when he was short of help. Dan was the best ship's blacksmith in that region, the stranger was told; and Doris had looked up, when her father said this, more pleased than Dan himself, who scowled and shook his head disclaimingly. Doris was evidently most penitent because she had offended this friend, and made shy endeavors to restore herself to favor; but she kept her seat by the window when he said good-night, and it was the kindly old farmer who held the flickering lamp high in the dark side doorway, while Dan lingered a minute wistfully, looking back once or twice, and then tramped away angrily down the yard. Doris thought she should see him in the morning, when he came to join the others; but though she was early at the landing, having insisted on her father's driving down, Dan had again crossed the meadows by the foot-path, and was gloomy and troubled all day as he cut and raked the grass. But Doris had done nothing wrong, she proudly told herself; Dan had no right yet to be master; while Dan considered himself more and more aggrieved, and so went presently to Sussex, and hammered away his wrath on the innocent bolts and bars of a fishing smack, but would not be merry or like himself, while many days went by.

Nobody could have prophesied such a complication of hindrances, but in all this length of time Doris could find no reasonable excuse for going to Sussex. She often drove in other directions with her father or with Mr. Dale, who had more than once asked to be transported whither his sketching instinct led him, but Sussex seemed to be forbidden ground. Once she would have gone simply because she wished; now there must be an indisputable necessity, evident to all beholders, and such, at last, was her mother's desire to inquire for the well-being of a cousin of whose illness they had chanced to hear. Dan was so old and dear a friend, she would certainly manage to see him, and to learn why he was behaving in this fashion. The color flamed in Doris's cheeks at the consciousness that he cared for her now in a new way; but it was strange enough that love, if this were love, should make him so impatient with her. All their lives long, they had differed more or less, and it never had separated them in the least. She had put him in her elder brother's vacant place, in her childhood. He had said once that he always meant to take as good care of her as Israel would have done.

But when Doris reminded herself of this, and wished that his feeling might never have changed, a sense of untruthfulness made the wish a not very compelling one. Mr. Dale had often spoken of going to Sussex, and Doris mentioned this to Mrs. Owen, to that good woman's intense satisfaction, and then serenely went her way to the studio.

"Sussex?" asked Dick, in a fretful tone. "Yes, that would be just the thing. I should like to see something new; I am tired of this awkward sham; and while you do your errand, I will try a sketch in one of those little ship-yards. I must n't scold at this, though, since you are kind enough to be pleased with it. Doris!" — He came a step nearer, and stood before her, looking at the white dress and at the apple-twig; then he gave a quick glance at her face. "Dòris, you really must not forget that I am going to make a sketch of you. Your father would like to have one to keep with your brother's, perhaps," he added. "I mean if I can make it good enough."

"Yes," answered Doris, ready to promise anything that day. "There would be nothing to prevent, almost any afternoon."

Dick took his brushes in his other hand. He was unusually smeared with his paints, and felt hot and cross again. Doris might have spoken so, if she had been a sort of picturesque gate-post or a sunflower; she must surely have understood something of what he meant to say; but at that moment she smiled, and was better to look at than ever. "I think you are tired," she said, in an altogether sisterly but quite charming manner. "You must take a whole day's vacation to-morrow, if we go to the ship-yards." But the thought of her secret made the least bit of a guilty blush flicker for one moment in her cheeks. Dan would be so angry, she thought, to see her coming with Mr. Dale, but she felt more than confident of her power of pacification.

X.

NEXT morning Mrs. Owen was in an unusually brisk and bustling frame of mind and body. She gave her daughter many important charges and messages, and treated the little expedition as if it were a most serious enterprise and a special embassy from herself. Dale half repented at the last, when he went to the studio to see his work and leave it in safety, lest a wandering breeze should overturn the easel, and break the corners of his treasured sketches. He liked the new picture now, and felt disposed to stay at home and go on with it, after all; but Doris was already waiting.

Mrs. Owen watched them drive away together with feelings of great pride. They meant to be home by dinner-time, for it was early yet, but who knew what might happen in the mean time!

As Doris had grown more and more anxious about her lover's non-appearance, she had become less self-conscious and more friendly with Mr. Dale, and this was readily mistaken by her mother for increasing interest. Lately the good woman had allowed herself to believe that propinquity, the cause of so many matches, was coming to the aid of this, and visions of Doris's city life and her own share in such real prosperity often delighted her. Sometimes she told herself that she was too old now and too far behind the times to take her part in the affairs of polite society, but the fact that her daughter would not be cut off from them and need not rust out on a farm almost made up for her own disappointment. A woman of more quick sympathies and perceptions would never have duped herself so completely. Outwardly, the frank good-fellowship of the two young people had been deceptive, and the sight of Doris driving her fleet young horse along the country roads, with Dale sitting by her side, had become familiar and most suggestive to more lookers-on than Mrs. Owen. The other farm horses were almost always used at that season, and Doris's had been unruly in its youth, and finally broken and always driven by herself. She was in the habit of going to the village to do errands, and it seemed the most natural thing in the world that she should often take the artist as passenger.

Dale carried a sketching-block and a brush or two in his hand, while his coat-pocket sagged heavily with the weight of his largest paint-box. There were some colors in it that he might need; beside, if he chose, he could stay all day at Sussex, and be driven home at night. It was more than an hour's journey, even at the quick rate the horse went, but there was nothing unpleasant in that thought. Doris was more than ever attractive, and her companion stole many glances at her. She was intent upon controlling the frolicsome horse; she looked eagerly at the windows of a neighbor's house; she thought of anything and everything, apparently, but the opportunity of taking a drive with Dick, whose efforts at conversation and successful jokes were only a part of the general excitement and delight of the morning. Doris was utterly unconscious of her own beauty, if an observer's opinion were to be trusted; her family also seemed to consider it of so little consequence that Dale sometimes wondered if he were deceiving himself, even while he had the delightful evidence before his eyes. It appeared to him that she made little use of her gift. Some women would lay waste and destroy, and others would be an inspiration to poets and painters; but Doris went her simple ways, dutiful, unselfish, and quiet, fulfilling her destiny with no regret at being defrauded of social gains or victories. She would have liked to escape a stormy wooing; if she should ever love any one, she wished the lover would understand, and say little about it to her or to any one else. The changes and events of life had always come to her naturally, as leaves push out of the bare trees in spring and flowers come into bloom. She did not like to speak her gravest and sweetest thoughts, or of her troubles, either; she was self-contained, and did not desire to be won through such harsh fashions. Dan ought to know that she had never thought of unkindness toward him. But now, if he were foolish and put out with her, she would surely go to see him and make it right. She had no coquetry, but she could avail herself of its weapons. She would tease Dan a little with the sight of Mr. Dale, and then undeceive him if he were deceived. Dear Doris! she turned toward Dick at that moment to see if he also had a mind to enjoy the morning's pleasure.

Love is forever a mystery; it is rooted deep in still greater mysteries, and the attractions and repulsions even of friendship are as inflexible as law can make them. Love and death are unknowable this side of heaven, but mankind is ever busy watching the signs of both with curious, unsatisfied eyes,— these strange powers that take possession of us against our will, and make us strangers even to ourselves. Dick Dale sometimes wondered afterward if this morning were not the time when a new motive and affection first took guidance of him. At any rate, he never before had been filled with a desire to kiss Doris Owen, often as he had looked at her lovely face. He was surprised at himself a minute later, but the wish was not to be forbidden so easily. The first leaf of that growth curled itself back into the soil again, having found the weather a little frosty for much flourishing, but the root was already strong, having taken several weeks now to fortify and spread itself unseen.

It was some distance across the sea of grass which surrounded the Marsh Island, and the free wind blew to and fro, as if it came from no particular quarter of the clear blue sky. The autumn haze had disappeared, and the outlines of the low country were clear-cut, and the bright, blurred colors of the vegetation strangely distinct. The bare hills, which reminded Dale very often of Northern Scotland, looked more astray than ever in the landscape. At all times of the year they seemed inharmonious and unrelated to the sea-meadows or fruitful upland slopes, as if some mistake had been made in putting together a great dissected map. Doris slowly turned her head as she glanced along the gray, sad hills. The least wild creature could hardly find shelter in all the distance; there was no reserve and no secret; the hills were like the telling of some sad, unwelcome news, in their harsh insistence and presence. "I used to be afraid to go over them when I was a little girl," she said. "I remember, after Israel died, father would stay there all day, sometimes. He used to say that he must mend the fences, but one day mother made me go and find him, and he just had his head in his hands, and sat there doing nothing. Poor father!" and Doris was silent again.

The marshes had faded since the day Dick Dale saw them first that year; their surface was soft and brown now, and even a cold gray where the grasses had not grown since the salt hay was gathered, — except that the shores of all the creeks were bordered with vivid green, so that the sombre coat of that part of the wide country was laced with green ribbons, and on such a day as this, when the tide was high, was also decorated with broad and narrow bands of blue, with crimson orders and noble decorations, embroidered here and there with samphire. The world was charmingly gay with all these colors and delights, but it was like a merrymaking in a tottering and defeated kingdom. A sadness hovered in the air; this was more like a commemoration of past glories than an inspiration and heralding of any that were to come. Dale was reminded, almost with pain, that he must leave his pleasant quarters before long; it would hardly be possible to stay at the farm in the winter; but he need not appoint the day for his departure now, thank fortune!

They stopped sometimes, while Doris spoke to an acquaintance, and often Dick could hardly help smiling at the quaint speech or the character of the conversation. He could not overcome the idea that Doris only played a part in such intercourse, that her natural instincts and experiences were of the sort he knew best, and that she looked at this rural life in his own fashion. He had discovered long before that the Owens were above the common level of society, and their character as a family bore much likeness to the uplifted Marsh Island itself. Doris really knew few people beside her own townsfolk. She had no idea of the vast number of persons with whom those who go much about the world may gain a half acquaintance. She often seemed, like her father, to have an insight into human nature which could have been secured only through some crafty and unnatural means. Yet their simplicity was the most marked thing about them,— their simplicity first, and then their generosity.

Dale had no idea of the real importance of the morning's enterprise. He concerned himself with his own pleasure, and enjoyed Doris's uncommon enthusiasm and excitement as if he were the inspirer of it; thinking once how she would grace a broader life than this, and that she deserved something better than Sussex and Dunster. He did not like her best clothes, simple as they were, so well as her plain house-frocks; he wished she would always wear the little dress of yesterday; but she never seemed quite like the tasteless and often tawdry young people he had been forced to associate with his remembrance of country neighborhoods.

Sussex came into view at last, — a white, irregular village, crowded close to the river, as if it had either made up its mind to embark, or had just come ashore. Doris's eyes brightened at the sight of her journey's end, and Dale's grew a trifle cloudy and disappointed. He would have liked to go driving on and on all that day, asking idle questions about the people and the houses along the road, and hearing a pleasant, clear voice answer him. There was something delightful in the very way her hands held the tightened reins, and one foot kept itself planted and braced. In fact, there was an admirable decision and purposefulness in the girl's manner which made her more interesting than ever.

It was after her usual manner of doing things that she faithfully performed her acknowledged errand first, and Dick was left for half an hour to his own devices, while she sat with the cousin inside an old gray house on the edge of the village. He would have been delighted to follow her, being curious to see if the interior were half as rewarding as he fancied, but he was not invited. He had decided only to look about the town that day, and to put in marks, as he expressed it; then he would come back again later. Dick had more work begun now than he was likely to finish; but as he sat before the old house which held Doris, and looked lovingly at its rain-colored, lichen-grown walls and the adorable traces of successive coats of green and yellow paint on its wide front door, he became again enthusiastic. Why would not every builder give his house one coat of red paint, and then leave all mural decoration to the weather? The very shutters on the inside of the windows were blotched and sunburnt into a semblance of mahogany, and the small, greenish panes of glass made delicious reflections in a sort of beckoning way at him. Yet the time went by slowly until Doris reappeared, and crossed the smooth, short grass toward the wagon. He had not observed the French pinks that grew near the worn doorstep until her dress brushed them as she went by; but then he saw, instead of looking straight in her face, as he would have done once, that a fresh tuft of flowers had blossomed on one of the fading stalks, and he could not help wishing to gather it for her. It might have bloomed at the sight of her, he thought, and then smiled in spite of himself, as he wondered what she would think if he told her such a sentimental thing. Once he had never hesitated at mentioning his pretty fancies, but it makes a great difference from whence a fancy springs.

"Are you tired of waiting?" she asked. "I am not ready yet. I must take my baskets in;" and by the time Dick had alighted to help her she had nearly reached the house with her burden, and laughed bravely at him a few minutes afterward, when she returned. He began to wonder what made her so merry. She was not laughing with him, neither did she seem to be exactly laughing at him, but the secret of her cheerfulness remained her own.

He had not remembered how picturesque and delightful the quaint town was. The high houses of sea-captains, the pride and circumstance of meeting-houses, the business of ship-building, and the almost Venetian privilege of water-ways won his heart completely. There was a long bridge, which seemed like a hawser that held the two parts of the town together, and stray seamen who lounged there in the morning sunshine spoke in voices that had caught some notes from the creak of rigging and sounds of wind and wave. Here and there a half-finished schooner pushed its bowsprit far ashore, and the incessant knocking of shipwrights' hammers was heard in a sort of rhythm, as they drove the treenails and fitted the stout planks, or more gently wedged in the wisps of oakum to keep the thievish water out. There was a strong flavor of tar and hard wood, a clean, dry odor, which contrasted with the dampness that rose from the black sides of the wharves and the sticky mud in the creeks. The tide was going out; the foundation of the village seemed to be insecure piles and slender sea-bitten timbers, between which one could look, as if they were great cages for long-since-escaped marine monsters. Olive-colored and brown sea-weeds clung to this old wood, while here and there was hanging a brilliant strand of green moss like floss-silk, shining and heavy with water. In the distance, a high white sail was slowly passing down the thoroughfare that led to the sea. From the rigging of an old schooner, under process of repair, the sharp, childish voice of a naughty boy was calling triumphantly to a troubled little sister below. A bright red flannel shirt — Dale never thought of the man who wore it — was wending its way slowly up the hill beyond the bridge. He did not notice in the least that they were so near a blacksmith's shop, or that they could hear the decided clink and ring of a heavy hammer upon an anvil, while Doris had looked for nothing and listened for nothing else.

Dick wondered why Doris stopped the horse in just that place. There were two large and rusty anchors and other small ones, and lengths of battered chain seemed to have been scattered about unnecessarily. Could she mean to have the horse shod by a ship's blacksmith? And then occurred to him the unwelcome thought that this must be Lester's place of business, which suspicion was confirmed directly by Lester's appearance in the doorway. He was scowling at Dale unmistakably, though he tried to be unconcerned; he did not look at Doris, who had begun to get down from the wagon. She took her foot from the step, however, and waited silently as he came toward them, stepping over the chains. His cheek was blackened by a careless touch of his smutted hand, and he had evidently been hard at work; where his shirt collar had lost its button and was falling open, the fairness of his throat made one imagine he had stained and darkened his face for some disguise. He swung his great hammer lightly, stood beside his visitors like a slender, vindictive Vulcan, and said carelessly, "Good-day, Mr. Dale. Any news, Doris?" as if he were only anxious to lose as little time as possible.

"No," said Doris, "there isn't any news;" and yet he would not look at her.

"Shall you be home this Sunday?" she asked softly, and was answered, with a quick glance from the blue eyes, that it was not likely. They were very busy with the schooner; some parties in Westmarket seemed to be in great distress for her. And at this pleasantry Doris took heart. "We were wondering what had become of you." But Dan Lester answered, in a tone that admitted no further conversation, that he was all right, and she must give his respects to the folks; at which Doris gathered up the reins quickly, turned the horse's head toward home, and departed.

There was a look in her face which Dale was not familiar with, and he did not see it then, though he felt it perfectly. He was sorry for the girl: he understood the morning's excursion well enough now, and would have liked to pound the surly blacksmith with his own hammer. Doris, for her part, felt as hard as a stone. She was rarely made so angry as this, and they drove homeward silently. A little later she told herself that Mr. Dale should not know that she had been defeated in the plan which she had made and cherished through so many happy hours. This was a quick and sorry ending, and she was as much grieved as angered. She thought nobody could tell that anything unusual had happened when she said, in a straightforward way, that Dan seemed to be busy that morning, and reached over to take a small basket from the floor of the wagon. "Will you eat a golden pippin?" she asked, with much composure, and chose one for herself, while Dick knew perfectly well that they had all been meant for Dan Lester.

They were outside the village now, and beyond the sound of either the clinking hammers or the knocking ones. A few minutes afterward they passed a school-house, and Doris scattered the rest of the apples by the roadside as she went slowly by, and laughed to see the children tumble together in a heap over them, while a little stray dog jumped and barked fiercely, as if he claimed a share. The teacher nodded to Doris from the doorway, and at that moment our heroine remembered that this person boarded at the same house as Dan Lester. " I suppose she will go straight home and tell him," thought Doris, more troubled than ever. There was a willfulness in the way things were going wrong. The teacher wondered why Doris blushed. It must have had something to do with Mr. Dale; but she need not feel so grand if she did get him to go to ride with her, just when everybody else was hard at work.

XI.

Doris's mother stood in the yard at least two minutes, in the bright sunlight, shading her eyes with her hand, and watching the young people drive away together. She was evidently much gratified with the sight, and nodded her head soberly as if in acquiescence, as she returned to the house. Temperance Kipp glanced at her superior officer once or twice with some curiosity, but said nothing.

The two women resumed their work, and the kitchen soon gave evidence of unusual industry. Israel Owen and Jim Fales, with the man called Allen, who had again been hired for a week, were to be away all day, finishing a piece of ditching which the farmer had planned in anticipation of the spring freshets. This was likely to be an undisturbed morning, and the good women had begun various enterprises, chiefly because they were sure of having the house to themselves.

If an outsider could have observed Temperance's honest countenance, he would have quickly understood that she was waiting for a good chance to say something to her companion. The relation between Mrs. Owen and herself was not recognized as that of mistress and servant except upon rare and inharmonious occasions. Ordinarily they looked upon each other as colleagues, and, to do her justice, the dependent was as heartily interested in the welfare of the Marsh Island and its inhabitants as any member of the family. Temperance was busy just now scrubbing some tin ware, a pile of which she had brought from the pantry, and worked away busily with soap and sand, sometimes holding off a big pan at arm's length to detect its imperfections. She watched Martha Owen cautiously, listening eagerly every time she spoke, but for some time answering her questions or remarks with a shade of disappointment or lack of interest. It was evident that she hoped to discern a frame of mind hospitable to some information she was ready to impart, or wished Mrs. Owen herself to introduce the subject of which her own mind was full.

But Mrs. Owen seemed preoccupied, and not so ready to discuss men and things as usual; she was busy now with her rolling-pin and flour-board at the farther end of the pantry, next the narrow window, from whence one could look across the flag-stoned court and up the hillside. This window opened only a little way; the two upper panes of glass were but half as tall as the rest, and the framework was absurdly heavy. The mistress had often threatened to have such a piece of antiquity replaced, though Dale had lately taken the trouble to make a sketch of it, with the curious outside coping or cornice. There were no two of the windows alike in that row at the back of the house, and some quaint, short curtains of old East Indian cottons were put there, where they would not often be seen and mocked. Dick had extorted a confession that there had once been a voluminous drapery of that really beautiful material for the best four-posted bedstead, and his hostess remembered now that she had promised to look among her possessions to see if there were not still a good piece of it. She smiled again at his admiration of the ugly old stuff that was so aggravatingly durable, and gave a more indulgent look than usual to the small curtain near by. "'T is pretty colored," she meditated, "but such a dreadful homely pattern. I do believe, if he had his way, he 'd set the old house back to just where 't was when I come here; old-fashioned as a dry-land ark."

Temperance saw the smile that followed this thought, and grew hopeful. "I expect they 'll find it pleasant getting to Sussex this forenoon," she ventured. "'T ain't so sightly along the ma'shes unless the tide is full." The whole family liked to have their country appear its best, and had constantly apologized to Dick for any defect in the weather.

"Yes," answered Mrs. Owen, thumping away at her pie crust, "they 'll have it pleasant, certain. Temperance," with renewed importance of tone, — "Temperance, why would n't it be a good plan to have up the stone jars, — the lard pots that 's empt'ed, and all them? We may not have such another good day, and 't is well to sun 'em out while we git a chance. Land, what a little while 't will be before we kill again! I never hear a squeal out o' the sty except

I think what a piece o' work I 've got afore me."

"Well," said Temperance, gathering up her shining pans to carry them out to the yard, " I did think of sweepin', but there 's no haste, and these tins were n't so bad as I thought for. I 'll take the stone ware next. I don' know, 'f I was you, as I would cross that bridge afore I come to it, about the hogs. 'T is a good three months yet." But Mrs. Owen responded with a somewhat ostentatious sigh, and abandoned herself to further reflection.

It was not until Miss Kipp had paraded her pots and pans in a beaming row along the garden fence that her opportunity arrived. "I declare, I never set out them lard and butter pots without thinking of pore Isr'el, that time he caught all the cats and kittens about the place, and shut one into each, and set the tops on, and I went and found 'em when I was going to take 'em in on account of a shower. I was dreadful put out, and I had to laugh, too. There he was a-watching of me from the woodhouse, and never dared to come in to his supper till going on eight o'clock. He wa'n't over six year old."

"I declare, I'd forgotten about that," said the mother. "I know one spell he used to play us plenty o' tricks," and she laughed a little, "him and Dan Lester. Do you know how they got some old clothes and things once, that was up garrit, and dressed themselves up, and come knocking to the door?"

"They'd made themselves to look like the minister and his wife," responded Temperance, with alacrity, "and I declare, you'd known they meant them anywhere. I'd no idea, though, when I see them first standin' on the doorstep, and I let 'em right in, for the joke of it, to where Parson Nash and his wife was setting, going to stop an' take tea. Land, how he laughed; but she was put out. Isr'el looked too much like her, and had just her walk and the way she held her head stepping up the aisle Sunday mornings. He said he did n't see who she was through them great spectacles. She went and got her a new bunnit afore the week was out. She was dreadful close. I don't think there ever was an amiabler man than the minister, though."

"I believe she's alive yet," said Mrs. Owen. "She had some money left her, you recollect, and I expect she'll live as long as she can, for fear o' somebody else getting it."

"There, now!" said Temperance Kipp, seizing this first chance and quite inadequate excuse for telling her secret, "I know I'm a-breakin' trust so to do, but when I wàs out last night I stopped in to Mrs. Lawton's, and she let on that they'd got expectations o' means above what she ever counted on. There was some land out West that old Lawton bought with some o' Dan's money. You know folks was always bejugglin' him into things. They've always paid taxes on it, no great till last year, and then it was ris', and Dan was awful pleased, but she expected him to be put out, and did n't dare show him the bill for quite a spell. He had sense to see 't was ris' in value, and now they've got word of the growth o' the place, and he's had an offer o' six thousand dollars down for it. She read the letter to me; it come day before yisterday, and she's been wantin' a chance to send it over. If Doris had been going by, I should have told her to call an' see if there was anything. But now don't you say a word, even to the 'Square. She made me give my pledge I would n't hint a word of it to nobody, but I thought I should bu'st if I had to keep it all to myself."

"I won't tell no secrets," said Martha Owen, doggedly, her black eyes shining, but not with pleasure. "I expect Dan 'll be the big man o' the town yet. I hope he ain't one o' them that's sp'iled if they get nine shillin's ahead. I used to like Dan when he was growing up, and him and Isr'el was so much together, too; but last time he come here I hoped 't would be some time before he favored us again."

"You had your wish, then," suggested Temperance good-naturedly. She had always liked Dan, and meant to do him a kindness in telling his good fortune. "I have a kind of notion that him and Doris have had a quarrel, and that she's going to make it up with him this morning over to Sussex;" and the adventurous handmaiden gave a sly glance across the kitchen.

Mrs. Owen never had openly declared her opposition. There were many reasons before Mr. Dale's arrival upon the scene why she had not cared to do so, and she restrained herself with a great effort now, though her face flushed, and the very expression of her broad back was vindictive as she bent over the table. "I don't know 's Doris need be in any hurry: she's well provided for as she is. And I want her to marry well when she does marry; but I expect she'll have her own way, and other folks must make the best of it."

"She'll never want to leave the farm, I don't believe," ventured Temperance. "I never see anybody have such a passion for anything as she has for the old place. Her father don't hold a candle to her, when all's said and done. Dan's wonted here, too, and would seem sort o' natural. I guess they'll make it up, fast enough," and she disappeared with another jar, while the mistress of the house wheeled about just too late, looking more angry than can be described; but when the placid countenance of Miss Kipp reappeared, Martha Owen had turned to the table again, and made no comment.

"I guess there's enough would snap at him if Doris lets him go for good and all." But this was putting patience to too great a strain.

"There, don't run on no longer, Temp'rance," said the mistress, contemptuously;

"you wear me out. There's plenty besides to concern ourselves with. I'm glad Dan's property is prospering," she added, generously; "but like 's not some starvin' lawyer out there wants a bid to do some work, and then 't will turn out to be a mistake."

Temperance held her peace. She would have liked to say more, but there was a decided barrier for the time being. She believed, herself, that Dan Lester was masterful enough to secure Doris, and it seemed an inevitable and proper thing that he should be the next owner of the farm. She was aware of the present mistress's fancies and ambitions, but she did not respect them much; they appeared to her unworthy of the judgment and experience of so sensible a woman. We have more patience with our friends' wickedness than with their foolishness, in this world; and for her part, Temperance thought the marriage of Doris and Dan Lester had been already too long delayed. She felt sure that a little encouragement and out-and-out talk about it were all that was necessary to precipitate so desirable a conclusion. But the mother, mindful of her daughter's beauty, though she had always striven, on fancied moral grounds, to betray no consciousness of it, and mindful more than most country women of the great world outside her own narrow horizons, was eager through Doris to come into connection with other society. She had always looked forward to a relation with better things, but she had made a common mistake in thinking these were wholly outward, and dependent upon anything but her own growth and development. The Martha Owen of the Marsh Island would be the same in whatever scenes or circumstances she found herself, and not transformed to match her new vicinity. A good soul, but stationary, it was a great pity she had not been wise enough to love the place where she had been kindly planted.

The morning went by. The pies were baked, and the pots and pans still a-sunning, and once or twice their guardian walked along the row, and tilted one more directly toward the sun, and gathered a few distracted grasshoppers from their prisons. She glanced down the road, and went to the outside of a window once to look in at the clock. The simple dinner was arranged for, and after this Martha Owen came out of the kitchen door for the first time since she had seen the wagon driven away, and went sauntering up the yard, much to the needless excitement of some idle hens, and finally, after a moment's hesitation and reflection, she climbed the short stairway to the spinning-room.

The little place looked very inviting; it was cool and quiet, and held an atmosphere of repose and reticence. The hot kitchen which she had just left kept too many associations with drudgery and monotony; and Temperance was in that mildly aggressive frame of mind which could not be too deeply resented. She was a faithful creature, was Tempy, but full of the notion that it depended upon herself to set the world right.

The apple-trees seemed to grow closer than ever about the windows. Their boughs were bending low with a great weight of fruit, and made the good woman sigh to think of the apple paring and drying which were near at hand. Doris knew only the favorable side of farm life, after all; she had chosen her work almost always, and every day there was some task that was lighter, pleasanter, than the rest. The mother's heart grew heavy as she pictured her only child growing faded and changed year after year, tired and worried more and more with the hard round and petty responsibility. Doris had it in her to grow beyond it all, as she herself had once; to do something else and something better; to be somebody, as she told herself with pathetic disappointment. Men folks were slow at understanding how a woman felt about such dull doings and lack of entertainment, the long winters and the endless, busy days of summer. She wished that Doris might be spared all this, even if Doris could grow fastest and be happiest in the very conditions which had fettered her own self.

The thought was suggested to her, as she surveyed the little room, that different uses might be made of the same materials. She could not help recognizing the charm of the place, although its furnishing was selected from her own disdained belongings. She left the three-cornered chair where she sat, and stepped about softly, glancing at the sketches which were displayed about the room. It was a strange thing to be looking at such familiar surroundings through another person's eyes, and she smiled at the likeness of one corner of the farm after another; the roofs and chimneys, the windows, the kitchen, the seldom-used front door, with the clustered rose-bushes almost blockading the way, and the row of bull's-eye panes of glass overhead. There was even the side of the small room where Mr. Dale still slept, with the sword over the narrow mantel-piece, and the table and chair near the window, and even the faint coloring of the landscape outside. She thought he must be some famous artist in disguise, as she saw the cleverness of the little pictures, all so amazing and impossible to a looker-on like herself. But most interesting of all was a diminutive looking-glass that hung on the yellow-washed wall, with a withered twig of cider-apples put into its frame. She had given him the mirror herself; the glass was spotted and dull, and she had been amused with his satisfaction and gratitude. Doris had worn the little apples in her belt the very night before, and he must have picked them up from the grass beside the door as he went up to the spinning-room that morning. She recognized them with a thrill of hope and pleasure. Somehow, she never had taken so good a look at the studio; she was not embarrassed now by anybody's presence. The young man's possessions were scattered about in luxurious disorder. Here was a well-browned pipe on the window-sill beside her, and a handful of letters which he had received the night before were lying on the seat of the nearest chair. She took up a book and opened it at a fly leaf, to see *R. Dale* written there in odd, twisted letters, and *Venice* underneath, with the date of a year or two before. He had lately been reading this foreign language, for one of his letters was between the pages, and Dick's new acquaintance looked at the strange words with distrust and suspicion. After all, how little they really knew about this stranger! He appeared to be a good fellow, but he might be poor and unsuccessful, — that is, poor for his station in life; and Mrs. Owen left the farm and the sketches far behind in her next adventurous reverie. Wonderful to relate, she thought with ever-growing interest of the news about Dan Lester's Western property. Temperance would have felt entirely rewarded if she had known how important her betrayed secret had become.

XII.

DAN LESTER had gone back to his anvil, had drawn an almost melting piece of iron from the forge, and beaten it until the sparks had flown across the shop to where one of the younger workmen stood, patiently filing and fitting a bit of steel. He called back angrily, and Dan did not notice him, but beat the harder and looked the crosser; finally he laughed aloud at nothing at all, and then whistled in a shrill and aggravating manner.

"Was n't that old Isr'el Owen's girl?" asked the apprentice needlessly. "Who was that furriner she was drivin' out? Some o' their folks?"

"No," snapped Dan; "'t was a painter fellow they 've taken to board."

"Kind of smilin'-lookin', 's if he was enjoyin' hisself this morning, wa'n't he? Pretty snug harbor there for one o' them swell gentlemen that lives by their wits," remarked the apprentice further, at the same time trying to shape a sharp jarring point of the steel with too coarse a file.

Lester dropped his own tools among the cinders, and strode across the shop to give the presumptuous youth a severe lesson in his trade; then he threw off his leather apron, and, taking some bolts as if he were going to the schooner, went out-of-doors. He felt as if the two or three men he passed on the bridge were laughing at his discomfiture, and grew more and more angry with Doris for having paraded her admirer through the town, and flaunted Dale in his very face. "I've made myself too cheap, that's a fact," growled Dan to himself. "I've waited on her year in and year out, and followed her about like a dog," and the tears filled the poor fellow's eyes. . . . He climbed to the schooner's deck presently, and was glad to find it deserted; he could not bear to be watched, and it was well that the workmen were down below, or out of sight caulking, or planing plank in the shipyard.

Dan leaned over the rail, and looked down at the white chips that covered the bank of the tide river. The shop had been hot and close, but here there was a fine fresh breeze from across the marshes, and presently his quick temper had burnt itself out like a straw fire. He found himself more sorry than angry after a few minutes of silence, and began to accuse himself of haste and unkindness. After all, what right had he to blame Doris Owen? She never had given a single sign that she loved or meant to marry him; she had never heard from his own lips that he loved her, though it was impossible to believe that she was anything but sure of that. How could she doubt it, when he had told her his love in every way that he knew beside speech! There might never be a chance to speak now, he told himself bitterly; he had been a fool all the time; but when you felt like a girl's brother and lover too, and had known her always, it was a great deal harder to begin your love-making. And then it might not have been Doris's fault that the artist came with her. Of course the fellow liked her, and was captured by her looks, and probably she had taken the first chance she could to come to Sussex, just as he hoped, though, after his fancied slight on that last evening, he had made up his mind to trouble her no further.

The wrath that had been kindled then had been smouldering ever since, though only that morning he had made up his mind to go home to spend Sunday. Now the ashes had shown their hidden spark, and the fire of his jealousy and pain had blazed ungenerously, and burnt away Doris's dear efforts at reconciliation.

She was gentle and serene, and undisturbed by small disasters; but her lover had learned through long association that her anger and prejudice were as slow to disappear as they were difficult to arouse. He was farther away from his happiness than ever, and all through his own folly. He fancied that Mr. Dale had looked at him with wondering disdain, and struck his clenched fist fiercely on the ship's rail at the thought. Poor Dan! he was very unreasonable. He looked haggard and old as he turned, in answer to a call from the bewildered and curious apprentice, who had been waiting for work until he was out of patience, in the middle of what had promised to be a busy morning.

Dan went on with his own work with less spirit than usual, though he joked and teased the undeceived stripling, for fear he should suspect there was any trouble. Once he leaned on his big hammer, and in the humility of his honest love reflected that Doris deserved a better man than himself. The stranger might be able to make her happier than any one else ever could. There was something very taking about Dale, though Dan himself never wanted anything to do with such a Miss Nancy. Old Mr. Owen thought he favored Israel, but Israel was worth two of that sort. It was not likely he would marry Doris, — that was the worst of it; he only liked to play with her; and by and by everybody would say Dan Lester was glad to get another man's leavings. No, he would go off out West, and make his way alone. There was that piece of land that was rising in value every day. He always meant to farm it some day or other, and to give up this makeshift of a trade. He would rather handle a good smooth live field and make it do its best than a lump of dirty dead iron. And at this the great hammer was swung aside angrily, and the crooked bar went to the forge again.

Visions of his broken plans came flocking up to tease him; his whole life had brought him steadily toward a certain goal, only to show him something like the brink of a precipice instead. In spite of the attempted kindness of his thoughts toward Mr. Dale, he could have stamped him into the dust after the schoolmistress had told him blandly, with a sidewise glance, at dinner-time, that Doris Owen and the boarder had stopped and treated the children to apples at recess-time that day, and they seemed to be having a sight of fun together. "They were splendid pippins," she added, indiscreetly, a few minutes afterward, to increase the effect of her first announcement. But Dan cast a contemptuous glance at her in return, and then felt shaky and accused himself afresh. Doris was bringing them to him. She always laughed because he liked them so much and hunted for them in the apple bins. Doris liked him now, if she had ever liked him, and he grew more eager to see her again, if only to know the width of the breach his ugly actions had put between them.

XIII.

LATE Saturday evening, Mrs. Lawton, Dan's mother, heard with great joy the sound of wheels in her narrow yard, and quickly taking a light, though the moon was at its full, she went to the side door. Dan greeted her with unusual cheerfulness as she asked, in a worn and feeble voice that contrasted poorly with his own, if he had received the summons she had sent him in the morning.

"I suppose you've got a split shingle on the shed-roof, or some such heavy piece of work," he answered. "Mrs. Dennell said you were all right yourself, so far as she could see."

The wagon shafts fell to the ground, and Dan was already clattering at the stable door; then the horse stumbled up the single step, and his master spoke to him now and then in loud tones, as he moved about, impatient with the delay of his supper. Mrs. Lawton still stood at the door holding the lamp, though the wind had blown it out some minutes before, when her son came toward her, along the moonlighted path. He laughed at the useless lamp, and the eager woman was filled with confusion; then they went into the small house together.

Dan threw his hat on a side table, pushed up a window, and seated himself beside it; the old cat came crying to his side, and not receiving at once the desired recognition, jumped into his lap and nestled down, purring loudly. Mrs. Lawton was busy trying to light the lamp again, but she let one match go out, and dropped another on the floor, and finally upset the match-box itself with a loud clatter. The moon shone into the room, and Dan looked round compassionately, and began to laugh at her disasters. She had not seen him in such good spirits for several weeks, and it was a great reward for her anxiety to have him at home again in such good trim. In her solitary, uneventful days, she had plenty of time to worry about Dan. Her past experience of life had certainly given good cause for some fear of the future.

"Never mind the light," he said; "it's bright as day here. Come and sit down, and don't flitter about so, mother; you make me think of a singed moth-miller. I've had my supper, you know. I did n't get away much before seven o'clock."

There was finally a successful attempt at illumination, and the little woman came toward her son and put her hand on his shoulder. "Now I 've got something to tell you, Danny," she said, and her voice was shaking with excitement.

The man's mind was filled with one thought, and something made him fear to hear news of Doris Owen and another lover than himself.

"Is Doris" — He spoke fiercely, but could not finish his sentence, and the mother's quick intuition possessed itself of his secret in that single moment.

"'Doris?'" she repeated, wonderingly; for why should he have thought of her then, even though he always thought of her most? "No. I had a letter from out West yesterday; that is, it came for you, and I did n't send it over. I was afraid something might happen; a letter is so easy to lose. That 's why I sent word, to be sure you 'd come home. It 's about that property Simeon invested some of your father's means in; it 's all of it yours, you know. They say it 's getting to have a great value. Poor Simeon,

I always thought he meant to do for the best."

Dan stood up suddenly, and the cat fell to the floor, much to her surprise and displeasure. "Where is the letter?" he asked.

"I'll find it in a minute. I put it somewhere so I could lay my hand right on it the minute you got here," and she made a fruitless excursion to her bedroom, which was next the room where they were. "I've found it!" she exclaimed at last, delightedly. "Here's the lamp." She stood beside him, watching his face while he read.

The letter was not long, and the young man smiled as he gave it back to her. "I should like more of the same sort," he said. "I'm not going to sell it, either, until I know more than this. They'd try to get the land as low as they could, and most like take advantage, if the owner was as far off as I am. I may have to go out there," he added, with a tone of pride and determination.

"I should take advice of Israel Owen," said the mother gravely. "You haven't had much experience in such things."

"Don't be fearful," said Dan, wishing all the while it were not too late to go to the farm that very evening. "I'm equal to managing my own affairs," he added, with feigned disregard of any such desire.

"Yes," said Mrs. Lawton, "you're all I could ask, my son. I shall be pleased to see you a well-off man. I haven't anything to hope for myself. You've kept me better than you need this good while. But there, it's natural you should be thinking about somebody else besides me." She sighed somewhat wistfully, and wished for a moment that she could always know that her son was her very own, and see no other woman caring for him and taking the first place. It was not very often they felt so near each other as they did that night, and she pushed back her chair to give him space, as he went walking to and fro, only a few steps each way, in the low room. He was a fine-looking fellow; any mother might be proud of him. Now he could live on his own place, and give up his trade, no matter if it were so enviable a place as master smith of the best ship-yard. Now he would be likely to marry. He was proud, Dan was, and had not meant, she was already sure, to speak to Doris Owen until he was independent.

"I wonder if Doris will feel pleased?" she said, almost unconsciously; and Dan stood still, with a smouldering light in his eyes, which looked black and stormy.

"I should have said so a month ago, mother," he answered defiantly; "but I don't know now. There's no telling about you women. I never have cared for nobody but her, though I've made no talk about it. I shouldn't to-night if you didn't speak first. If I can't marry her, I shall live single,— that's all; and the harder I have to work, the better. I shall want something to make me forget I've lost what I've always wanted. I'll let the money go hang."

The troubled and startled woman rose, and went quickly to her son's side. Dan sat by the square table, and had dropped his head on his arms. She patted his shoulder with a light hand that trembled a little; somehow, her pleasures were apt to have a bitter ending and go wrong. She wondered if he were crying,— Dan never cried; but presently she heard a sob, and the broad shoulder shook under her touch. "Don't, dear, don't!" she whispered, anxiously; "'t will all come right. You're just like your father, and I couldn't have said him nay. Girls will be girls, Dan, and she's waiting, most like, for you to speak. There ain't a thing that's unworthy about Doris. She favors the Owens, and I know 'em root an' branch."

Dan looked up presently. His eyes were blue again, now, and when his mother's hand had stroked his hair, and he felt the worn, thin fingers touch his neck, it had sent a thrill of comfort to his very heart. Poor little mother! He stooped down and kissed her as tenderly as if she were Doris, before he went to bed. "Faint heart never won fair lady," he said, and tried to laugh; but her shock of delight and surprise at his unwonted caress reflected itself back to him, and as he stood looking down at her, his own eyes were suddenly and provokingly blurred. She was so little and frail in her scant old dress, and had such a patient, hard-worked look; he remembered that people said she had been a pretty girl. He wondered if he had not been too rough for her sometimes; she was the kind of woman that cannot stand alone, and wants to be taken care of. Confound old Lawton, who made a drudge of her! But Dan all at once understood why the lonely woman had been persuaded to yoke herself to him. After all, this piece of land might serve a good turn. And Doris,

— was she really waiting for him to speak, after all? What a fool he had been! Her eyes had sought his face pleadingly when he went snarling to the wagon to speak to her.

It was long to wait until the morrow; and the white, bright moonlight kept him awake, as if some fate insisted on prolonging the delay. The wind was blowing a little, and a lilac bush outside brushed against the clapboards just as it did when he was a boy. Sometimes, even then, he used to lie awake and think of Doris Owen, and he remembered a dream which had seemed very real: for the boy Israel, his dear playmate, had come to him, — not in his soldier clothes, but wearing his old school-boy jacket and boyish face, — and stood by the bedside, and begged him to go and live at the farm. Dan Lester had gone to the war, too; he had seen his playmate fall, and had dragged him back within the lines at the peril of his own life. His thoughts were rarely so busy as in this still night, as he grew by turns hopeful and fearful of his fate.

XIV.

EARLY the next morning, Dale disappeared from the farmhouse, meaning to spend most of the day out-of-doors. Doris's boat did not usually leave its anchorage on Sunday, so he borrowed it without hesitation, and drifted seaward with the ebbing tide along the winding highways of the marshes, changing his point of view just fast enough, and idly watching the clouds and the landscape in his slow progress. He was not uncomfortable, leaning back against an oar which he had put behind him across the boat, and he wielded the other oar skillfully to push the light craft off the shore, against which it not seldom came to a full stop. The country was brilliant with autumn tints, and often the glimpses of it were charming to his eyes; for the water was low in the creeks, and the black mud at the sides, topped by the still luxuriant bending grasses, made a pleasant framing. The day promised to be hot, but it was cool weather in the deep channels, and he had a sense of being sheltered and hidden securely. The great dragon-flies followed him, as if they had left everything in their surprise and excitement, and sometimes three or four alighted together, glistening against his dull-colored clothes like fairy marauders in full armor. As he leaned over the side of the boat, the small fishes and occasional crabs did not seem disturbed by the gliding shadow; they might have thought it a natural part of their calm existence, until the plash of an oar sent them off in alarm. After half the morning was spent, this leisurely navigator found himself fairly stranded at an absurdly short distance from the Marsh Island; but the tide being almost out, there was nothing to do but to go ashore and wait for it to rise again. The bank sloped conveniently, and he scrambled up and providently pulled the light dory after him, and fastened the painter to a bush. He had often looked across from the farm uplands to this smaller island in the salt grass; but it was larger than he had fancied it, and the beech and oak-trees had reached a good size, and were dropping their ungathered nuts into the thickets and coarse grass beneath. Two or three squirrels scolded at him from a safe distance. He seated himself in the shade, and looked across the level reaches of the sea-meadows, which had begun to shimmer in the summer-like heat. The small beech-trees that grew near made the light purple and soft that fell on the frayed whitish carpeting of their last year's leaves, and presently he grew drowsy, and turned over to put his arm under his head; and there he lay, sound asleep, at his lazy length, — a fair, untroubled knight, one would say, though his mind had lately perplexed itself harshly enough.

The country wagons had just rattled churchward along the East Road, their two seats crowded full for the most part, with small children wedged between the grown people, much hotter than was comfortable already. For a wonder, Doris had pleaded fatigue, and announced her intention of staying at home. It was a long drive to the village, and Israel Owen and his wife decided to spend the noon at a cousin's, as was not infrequently their custom. Temperance Kipp always passed the day of rest with her sister, and Jim Fales had gone to his mother's, a mile or two away. Doris would keep house, she said. There was always a cold lunch at noon on Sundays at the farm. Nobody knew when Mr. Dale would be likely to return, and the unused horses had been led out early to join their four-footed companions in the pasture. There would really be nothing to do. Martha Owen looked over her shoulder once or twice at Doris, as she drove away. The girl seemed unlike herself, and had been pale and intent ever since she came home from Sussex, though she answered her mother's questions about the expedition, and even her interview with Dan Lester, with her usual frankness. The more the elder woman revolved in her mind Temperance's bit of news, the more respect she was inclined to pay it. Dan Lester was almost like one of themselves already, though she had not been pleased with him of late; he would be very well off now. The castles in the air, of which she had fancied young Dale the ruler, began to betray their unsubstantial foundation, and Dan's cause ventured to assert a likeness to the bird in the hand which is valued by all persons of discretion. And when, at a cross-road, they met Dan in his shining new buggy, driving his mother to meeting, Mrs. Owen gave him a most friendly salutation.

Alas that Dan, disappointed at seeing the vacant place on the front seat beside the kind old farmer, should have fancied the greeting to be one of exultation and defiance, or approval of the fact that Doris had stayed at home, to enjoy the artist's company.

Doris had seen Dick Dale turn to the eastward as he went up through the orchard, and instinctively set her own face to the westward when she also wandered out-of-doors. The house had seemed hot, for a wonder, and the crickets and their relations of the harsh voices chirped and hissed with August-like fervor outside the windows. She tried to read, but presently the paper slid to the floor, and as she passed out of the door the old clock ticked louder than usual, as if it were calling her back: "Don't — Do — ris — don't — Do — ris," but she willfully went away, for all that. She did not like the stillness of the old place, — an empty house of that age grows full of the presences that are felt, but not seen, — and she kept on her way steadily up the hill, and left the doors open behind her, so that whoever chose might go in and keep holiday.

This was true, that she felt the vague pain and sense of discomfort which are apt to foretell the great changes of our lives. She wished that her existence might have swept on in the familiar fashion of which she had never complained. Was love a happiness, or life a satisfaction, or friendship a certainty, if Dan Lester, whose affection had been so constant and so evident, could doubt her and shame her before a stranger? The gentleness and courtesy of Mr. Dale himself might be safer qualities to rely upon. She had neither promised Dan anything nor given him cause for jealousy. There was no need that he should call to her in the way he did before the haymakers, that night at the landing, but she had been sorry enough if she had shown unkind resentment. Indeed, she could think of a dozen times when she had spoken with more impatience, and even slighted him and teased him far more. Why could not people be more generous to you when they loved you than when they were simply friends? She could not forgive Dan's surliness. If she had cared less for him, she would not have gone to him there in Sussex; and the blood crimsoned her cheeks at the thought of such undeserved humiliation. The natural instinct that had waited and reached out unconsciously for a lover was wounded and thrust back, to be recognized with shame and sorrow. Doris Owen was a woman who would be comparatively useless in a solitary life. Hers was a nature incomplete without its mate, and incapable of reaching its possible successes alone. She had been more ready to make the great choice than she thought, and nearer the solution of the problem which now seemed entirely new and strange. Perhaps it was necessary that she should apparently take a step backward and approach the crisis again before consenting irrevocably to her fate.

Doris felt rather than thought these things as she climbed the easy ascent; she would have been too much shocked if her true ideas had been put into words. Where the hill grew steeper, she changed her direction, and left the shade of the great apple-trees to go through the peach orchard. Here the sunshine was steeping everything through and through; the fruits stored it away, and in return gave out into the air something of their fine fragrance and mellowness. The slender trees were filled with a rare vigor and elasticity, and held up their too heavy burden of half-faded leaves and delicate laden branches as if they were getting a new lease of life. The thick grass was spotted with brilliant windfalls, and bees went buzzing by, rich with their plunder from this late harvest. Doris walked lightly among the company of trees, and presently her drooped head was also lifted up, as if the kind sun had drawn and strengthened it, and her face began to free itself from clouds, like a clearing sky. A fair young girl of out-door growth and flower-like fashioning, a sweet-faced wife for any man to win and cherish, she passed fleet-footed over the autumn grass. Her light dress flitted between the peach-trees and hid itself behind the hedge-row of hazel-nut bushes and young wild-cherries. At last Doris stood on a high slope, a white figure against the blue sky, where the sea-breeze found her; and since the inland country looked warm and inhospitable, this zephyr turned, and went no further.

There was no reason why she should go back to the house for a long time yet. Her half-outgrown childish love of wandering far and wide took possession of her, and remembering all in a moment that the beech-nuts on the small island nearest her must be nearly ripe, and that the tide was out, she went slowly down the pasture and across the marsh. She had told Mr. Dale once that she thought the most beautiful time of the year was the late spring, when the marshes were growing green, but her own countryside never had seemed more delightful than it did that Sunday morning. She questioned, with pain and foreboding, if she must ever leave it. She put aside so needless a fear, and was grateful to the stranger within the gates for teaching her by his own delight to see the beauty that she had never half understood. Doris wondered where he had gone, — he was sure to be keeping one of the ten commandments and doing no work. . . . They could not be too thankful to so kind a friend, who valued their friendship and service beyond what it was worth, and returned it in every way thrice over. He was like the young men in the best stories that Doris knew, — she had often told herself that, — and her heart gave a little flutter of uncertainty. Poor Dan! he was really just as kind at heart and full of pleasant thoughts; but he was a country fellow, and lacked the ways of the world and the gift of ready speech. She could not think what had made him behave so strangely, and the recent hurt began to ache again.

The noonday sun was very hot, after all, and she was glad at last to reach the shelter of the spreading trees of the little island. The young beeches at the edge of the thicket were turning yellow, but inside they were untouched by frost or ripening. The oaks were dull red here and there on the outer branches, and Doris laughed at a squirrel which felt it necessary to perch on a fallen tree and menace her with whisking tail and indignant chatter. The squirrels had always acted as if this island were their own ; it was a favorite trapping-ground of Israel's. She gathered some late blackberries, as she went pushing her way through the tangle ; she well remembered a grassy place under the largest beech on the seaward side, where the air might be cooler. Just as she could look out through the drooping boughs at the bright, hot levels beyond, she was startled at the sight of the bow of her own small white boat with the blue stripe, drawn up on the bank of the narrow creek, and here, almost at her feet, lay Mr. Richard Dale, sound asleep.

She turned instantly, but the rustle and cracking of the bushes had waked him. He sprang to his feet, looking quite stupid and amazed, and slowly caught a spider that was spinning down from his hair. Then he regained his wits entirely, and looked at his disturber with a laugh. "Where did you come from, Doris?" he asked. "You must have taken the hay-boat; the other was gone, so I had to steal yours. The tide must be quite out by this time."

"The tide is coming in," said the girl. "I must hurry back, or I cannot cross some of the low places. I walked over the marsh; it isn't very far, and easy enough if you only know the way. When the tide is half high, you must take a longer way round."

"I should lose myself, at any rate," answered Dick; "at least, I should never escape by land. There is something mysterious about the marshes to me. Sit down," he said, more gently. "How hot it has grown! Why not wait until the creek fills again, and we can go back in the boat together? I am by no means sure I know the way;" at which they both laughed, and felt more at ease. Dick shook himself like a wet dog; he was adorned with dead leaves and bits of twig, and sleepy yet, if the truth were told. Then he sat down on the grass, and Doris followed his example, and as she leaned back against the beech-tree's broad trunk, she was not displeased with the unexpected turn of affairs. Dick picked up a sound beech-nut that some squirrel had dropped by mistake, and, cutting off one of the trig three-cornered sides, offered it to his guest.

"I wish I had brought some peaches," she said. "I just came through the orchard."

"It was very odd that we both should have come to this same spot of ground," the young man observed meditatively. "Sometimes I think there are all sorts of powers and forces doing what they please with us, for good or bad reasons of their own."

"We are taught to believe that one power is, are n't we?" asked Doris timidly. "But always for our own good."

"Yes," slowly assented Dick, as if the fact were not always so clear to him as he wished; and then, with renewed interest, "I always liked the notion of our having guardian angels. I should like to know if it is true?"

Doris flushed: she was not used to talking in a familiar way of such grave subjects, but she could not help answering, "I always have thought so ever since I was a little girl," she began hesitatingly. "It always seems as if there were one angel who follows me all the time, and tries to keep me back when I am going to do wrong, and is set to take care of me. Don't you know" — and she became very earnest — "that when you forget things, or can't remember where you leave things, something outside yourself reminds you? Not your memory or your conscience; something outside you," Doris repeated. "I wonder if we don't have friends in the unseen world."

"Perhaps," the young man said gravely. "I really don't know why not." He was touched by the strange beauty of Doris's face now when she was deeply moved. She was paler than usual, even after her walk; she was like another creature from the busy week-day girl who went and came with the elder women at the farmhouse. She almost always had a grave sweetness. There was surely a most uncommon quality in both her nature and her father's.

"Doris," said Dick, in a brotherly way, "I think you did not like me when I first came to the farm."

Doris was silent. Then he glanced up, to find her looking at him with surprise and bewilderment; it might have been because she was called back unkindly from some reverie.

"I did not know you," she answered. "I hardly thought about you until you hurt your foot. But we are all so glad you came, now; it has been a great deal of company for father, and mother gets very tired of doing the same things over and over. I think she would like to live where there is more going on."

"Would you like that, too?" asked Dick softly, and then was persuaded that Doris's belief in a spiritual guardian was well founded; he felt such an unexpected sense of remonstrance.

"No, indeed," answered Doris simply. "I like home better every year;" and suddenly an invisible quality in the air, a subtle intoxication that had something to do with Dick's question, sent its influence into Doris's heart, and for the first time she could not look Dick in the face. She wondered how she might escape, not so much from him as from her appalling self.

There was a terrible silence, and the longer

it continued the more convicting it grew. Dick Dale did not speak again, — he did not know what hindered him; in that moment his heart beat very fast. Was Doris waiting to hear his voice? Was this his fate and happiness, and was his future in this woman's keeping?

The breath of enchantment was quickly gone, and they became their familiar selves again, yet with a difference. Dale, at any rate, felt a faint sense of mistake and disappointment, and went away without a word when Doris said that she thought they must go back now, if the boat would float in the creek. She looked at him appealingly as he helped her to her place, and only smiled when he demanded the oars which she had taken.

"I have not rowed for a long time," she said in excuse, and pulled with strong, steady stroke, as if it were a relief and welcome defense against threatened discomfort. "You would not know the meadows in winter," she said once. "They look so dead and desolate, with great black cracks in the ice, like scars; and at night you can hear a noise as if the tide were caught and trying to get itself free. I am always so glad when the gulls and crows are thick, and it is getting near to spring."

"No," said Dale to himself, "I don't believe I could stand the long winter. Town is the place when the snow comes." But he wished, none the less, that he could make the winter delay its coming. He did not like to have Doris row the boat, and a great insecurity and indecision took possession of him. Should he dare to speak to Doris? He wondered what he would think of it tomorrow; but he called himself a coward, as they landed a little later, and he walked back to the still-deserted farmhouse by her side. The old place had arrayed itself against him while he had been away. He felt curiously distinct and separate from his surroundings just then, and yet as if he must use all his powers of resistance if he would keep himself apart. Did fate mean to graft him to this strong old growth, and was the irresistible sap from that centre of life already making its way through his veins? Was an unlocalized, a disestablished human being at the mercy of a possible system of spiritual economies, so that he was to be held to a spot that was lacking in what he might supply? If a man did not see his duty and opportunity with his own eyes, must he be attracted by a magnet-like necessity? But what was this broken, nay, even mutilated, household to him, even though the strange suggestion of his likeness to the young soldier who lay in the orchard burying-ground would flit through his bewildered mind? There was a new glamour over everything: at one moment he reveled in it, and then as suddenly feared and distrusted it, while a faint indignation returned again and again and troubled him because he had been thus taken by surprise.

All the time that Dale's thoughts were attacking him like an angry and desperate mob, Doris walked at his side, so sweet and self-possessed, so staid and Sunday-like, that her presence was the only thing that quieted the confusion she herself was making. Never before had this girl looked so slender and full of life, so kissable and dear. Presently she turned toward him with almost perfect composure; there was only a little look of affectionate solicitude to show that they had just come a long way nearer each other's consciousness.

"I will go up to the orchard and get some peaches for your lunch, Mr. Dale," she said. "The best ones are just getting ripe;" and

Doris went away slowly up the hillside, through the long autumn grass, into the shadow of the fruit-trees. Dick could not follow her, but for some minutes he stood still. What a picture for a man to paint! What a woman for a man to love! Ah, if Doris had looked over her shoulder in that minute! But the white dress was lost among the shady apple-trees, Dick sighed, and well he might; the enchantress had passed by, and her spell had passed with her. An eager song-sparrow flew upward, singing bravely, and for once the blessed notes jarred upon the young man's ear.

He climbed the stairs to the spinning-room. The light southwesterly wind sent a cloud of cigar-smoke through the northeasterly window after a few minutes, and as Doris came down the hill she saw this, and smiled. A little later she brought some bread and a blue plate full of great crimson and yellow peaches, and put them on the table. Dick, who held a book in his hand, nodded, and thanked Doris politely, but she had already turned away. She was hardly at the foot of the steep stairway before he had left his chair and dropped the book on the floor. He stood still, eager, irresolute.

Was he a fool or a wise man? — but he saw her no more that afternoon. There was enough else to do. He had letters to answer, for one thing; but Dick could not write; he kept making dots and squares and curious little marks with his pen all over the blotting paper, instead. Neither could he read, for he heard the ripe apples fall to the ground, and saw a gray spider spin its web and lie in wait for flies. At last he heard the elder Owens drive into the yard, and bravely appeared as a listener to the news they had brought home from meeting. A strange pleasure filled his heart at the sight of Israel Owen's honest face. The good man seemed more familiar to him than he did to himself.

XV.

SUNDAY evening was apt to be given to social advantages at the Marsh Island. The farmhouse had been for many years a favorite gathering-place of the few neighbors, and in the old days the Owens' tall clock had served as a frequent and formal excuse for the appearance of various sociable acquaintances. A clock of such high rank must necessarily rule all timekeepers of lesser degree by the autocratic sway of its leisurely pendulum; and once in a while somebody would still ask, with noticeable humility, for the right time, or set the hands of a cumbrous silver watch, by way of tribute, in the clock-room.

The elder Owens, Israel and Martha, with Temperance Kipp, returned tired and dispirited from their day's devotions, but a comfortable early supper had refreshed them; and Doris had seemed so entirely like herself that when Dick Dale came strolling up from the garden with his cigar, and heard the sound of voices, he joined the cheerful company without a moment's reflection. A luxuriant growth of petunias, still unhurt by frost, had made the old garden deliciously fragrant, and in the dim light he could see the flowers' pale faces glimmering at his feet. He picked one which gained his special attention, and gave it to Doris as he entered the room. A heavy dew was falling outside, and the company, for almost the first time that autumn, had forsaken the broad side-door step altogether. When Dick had first come to the farm, his presence had been a serious hindrance to the undisturbed flow of mild discussion and neighborhood news, but now, after a slight pause and cordial greeting, he was allowed to seat himself by one of the windows without note or comment. Old Mrs. Bennet, the last arrival, was still out of breath, and presently explained to the new-comer that she always used to walk the distance between her house and this in ten minutes, easy; but now she had to hurry along, in order to accurately compare the difference of the clocks.

Temperance Kipp regarded Mr. Dale with keen eyes. She had taken up the neglected championship of Dan Lester with more decision than before, since she had seen his discouraged face that morning in church. He looked thinner than usual, and altogether was very appealing to her tender heart. Even the news of his increase of fortune had not made him light-hearted, though his mother had exchanged a confiding and pleased glance with her old friend, as she sat in one of the side pews, not very far away.

Dale watched Temperance herself with uncommon pleasure that evening. He had always liked her face, which had a great deal of sympathy and wise understanding in it; for the first time he recognized a resemblance, which had always baffled and puzzled his memory, to Holbein's portrait of Sir Thomas More. He was a little amused and surprised at this; he would have liked Bradish to see her, as she sat in a high-backed rocking-chair. Bradish was very fond of the Holbein. "Ah, well, I must be getting back to town soon," the young man assured himself, and then moved his own chair a little, as if he wished to hear what was being said of the morning's sermon, but in reality to command a better view of Doris. He was not infrequently bored by the theological disputes of Israel Owen and his neighbor Churchill, who was a received authority on some questions, being a deacon of the first parish. This controversy was evidently almost over with. "Speakin' about the Lord knowin' them that are his," said Israel Owen, in an unsteady voice, " it makes a good text to enlarge upon for a minister ; but when you come to put it right home, deacon, there 's precious few for him to know. Folks ain't so common that bears him any great likeness that he can make friends of. Plenty of us is growing towards him, and kind of stirring about some; but it 's a mercy, as I view it, that we 've got another life to continue the upward way. If we can only git started whilst we 're here, that 's about all we can do, most on us."

The deacon grumbled something, which might be an assent, and might not. His own preference was for more inflexible condemnations and harsher definitions of the condition of fallen man ; but somehow he never could bring his arguments to bear when Owen took this tone. " I don't wonder, when I look about me, that folks ain't better," the old man concluded ; " the 'stonishment to me is that they ain't wuss. When you take in what folks have inherited down from gineration to gineration, and how some are weak in body and some in mind, 't is a wonder a good many is so decent behaved as they be."

But the deacon did not like to think of the practical achievements of himself and his brethren, — the abstractions and distinctions of certain doctrines were a much better liked subject; and he was relieved when a tall figure appeared in the doorway, and Dan Lester looked in, with a touch of defiance on his face.

"Come in, come in, Dan!" said the farmer. "Where 've you kept yourself these weeks past? I did n't know but you was put out about something. Did n't overdo, haying, did ye? I 've hardly seen ye since. Doris, git Dan' a seat. We've got consider'ble of a meetin' here, but there 's chairs enough. Step out to the entry, Doris, or fetch one right in from the kitchen."

Doris had risen at the guest's approach, and they stood together in the room for one awkward minute, with the rest of the people watching them. It takes little time for such a neighborhood to scent out the smallest excitement; and the curiosity to know if there were anything between Doris and Dan of an unpleasant nature, or any prospect of a love affair between her and Dale, had led two or three of the guests to pay this evening visit.

Dick Dale had sometimes been vastly entertained by such a Sunday evening gathering. He liked the quaint talk and picturesque expression of the elder people, and had more than once wished that he were a writer, and could profit by the specimens of a fast-disappearing dialect. This night, however, there was a strange influence of excitement and expectancy. He was inclined to resent Dan Lester's coming to the farm in that self-sufficient way, after his late treatment of Doris. He knew well enough that she had been grieved by it. Dear Doris, what a shame it would be to let her waste herself among such unappreciative people ! He should like to hear what some of his acquaintances would say if they saw her, — and this irate admirer proposed to himself to go out-of-doors again, yet lingered, because it might appear that he was unfriendly to his rival.

"They always came to our funerals," Mrs. Bennet was saying, in a reproachful, low voice to the other women, " but they kind of hung off about it, too, and did n't step right to the front and jine in at such a time, as the Maxwells did, and others. 'T ain't what I call being related to folks."

" They ain't folks; they 're nothin' but a pack o' images," proclaimed Temperance Kipp, in a tone that admitted no contradiction.

Dick laughed at this; the other listeners turned their heads to look at him half suspiciously, yet with great good humor. Presently, seeing that the full moon must be near its rising, he left his seat by the window, and went out. He did not notice the appealing glance of Mrs. Owen; in fact, there was no trace of any such feeling in Dale's heart as that of being driven off the field. He was simply doing his own pleasure, and leaving the good souls to theirs. A minute afterward there was a shout of laughter from the clock-room which made him wince. One naturally thinks one's self the injured subject of mirth at such a moment. Then, as he turned, he saw two figures come out of the door-way, Doris and Dan Lester, who had sat just inside, and who were also tempted to stroll out into the soft night air. As Dick looked and listened, the old farmer and his crony moved their chairs into the square side-entry, and the women passed to and fro in the clock-room, as if they were drawing nearer together for a season of gossip.

The great willows made huge masses of darkness against the starlit sky; the lights in the house cast a network of long shadows before their rays. Dick Dale leaned upon the garden fence, and watched the yellow harvest moon as it rose above the misty shrouding of the earth. The outline of the hill looked hard and more distant than the moon itself. He could hear a faint sound of the sea and an occasional laugh from the house. By and by Doris and Dan came back again. The grass had been wet the way they went, but indeed they seemed indifferent to their surroundings, and went walking to and fro, while the resentful spectator kept his chosen station. He thought that anybody might see him who looked that way, being as conscious of his own presence in the landscape as if it had been broad daylight.

Even Doris, who knew every outlook so well, did not see that any one stood this side of the withered sunflowers. She wondered once or twice which way Mr. Dale had gone; but since his lameness was cured, he had often been out until late in the evening, and let himself into the house after every one else was asleep. He was a revelation to her in many ways, with his knowledge of books and his love for nature. She felt a sense of wider liberty with Mr. Dale than with any one else she knew, and believed in the possible treasures of experience and knowledge that lay far beyond the horizon that she was able to discover.

To-night Dan Lester was very gentle, almost pathetic, but strangely compelling. As he came into the room, earlier, her heart gave a great bound of relief and affection. Now, as he spoke with eager impatience, as he stood close beside her, and she could just see his familiar features and mark his height against the dim western sky, she would have been thankful to find a way of escape. She did not stop to question his right to call her to account, neither did she answer him when he humbly condemned his own wrong-doing of the day before. Yes, he loved her; there was no doubt about the truth of his faithful kindness to her, or his endless care and tenderness, — she knew that without his telling it so tempestuously. She wished he would cease his entreaties. She could not speak in reply; she felt dumb before her inevitable fate when Dan told her of her father's favor toward him, weeks ago, as they were on the south marsh together, one August morning.

The lover's story did not touch her, after all; it seemed quite outside her heart, and could not find a way in. Doris grew more and more weighed down with a sense of this grave business. She felt a strange impulse to throw herself into poor Dan's brotherly arms, and beg him to defend her, as if this distress had come from any one but himself. A vision of Dick Dale's boyish face, with the strange, sweet look it had worn for an instant that day, came to her mind, and gave her a fancied courage and protection. She turned away from Dan with a sigh and feeling of reprieve. "Don't think hard of me, Dan; there's time enough," she faltered, and then hated herself for so heartless a wording. "I must go in. No, don't keep me, Dan. I do think everything of you. I always have" — and the girl's heart felt as if it would break with sorrow and despair.

Strange to say, she did not think of Dick Dale any more, but of Dan himself instead. She wondered if he would speak again. Her heart softened, and though he had gone away a step or two she felt as if he were drawing her toward him through the darkness.

Then a thin figure appeared beside them, and hesitated, as if reluctant to intrude. "I guess you two had kind of dry scratchin', coming up the crick this mornin'," said Jim Fales, by way of pleasantry; "tide was pretty low when I see you. I set out to cross over and tell you to land on the pint where the big pitch-pine is; it ain't much further to walk, when the ma'sh is dry;" and he hurried on, being later than was his wont, and anxious to report to his employer.

Doris could not say a word. Dan Lester muttered something under his breath, and strode away. The girl looked after him, took a few steps as if she meant to follow him; then she stood still. "Oh, Dan, Dan!" she whispered, almost aloud. "He is so quick; what made me let him go!" But as love and pride fought together in her perplexed mind, the footsteps were gone out of hearing, down the long road, the long, long road, into the dreary darkness.

Later, the moon was round and bright in the sky; the cheerful sound of voices grew louder, and the guests were making ready to depart. "I guess the young folks is philanderin' off somewhere," said Mrs. Bennet, as she stood on the doorstep. Doris met her bravely, but she was not good at dissembling, and lingered in the shadow outside the door. Dan had gone home, she told the waiting audience; he had to be off early in the morning, as they knew. But Temperance grumbled that he might have said good-night, coming as seldom as he had lately. She looked narrowly at Doris's pale face, and resolved to have a talk with her before they slept. As for Doris's mother, she began to wonder if the girl had been foolish or hasty. Dan would be well off now; and after all, Doris would never like any place so well as the farm, — the love for it was born in her. Dan had treated Mrs. Owen very civilly as he came in, but he was resenting her smiling salutation of the morning more than ever at that moment, if she had only known it.

Later still, Dick Dale appeared. The night was growing very damp and chilly, he told his friends. He wondered what Lester had asked and what Doris had answered, but Doris was nowhere to be seen. The farmer was fastening the doors and windows. "We used to leave everything open in warm weather," he said, "but times have changed since the war. Good-night, my lad!" And so that day was ended.

XVI.

NEXT morning the farmhouse seemed quite unlike the scene of an excitement of any sort. The walls kept many a secret already, and the old homestead concerned itself only in providing a shelter and resting-place for its children. Mrs. Owen was singing one of yesterday's psalm-tunes in a high, energetic voice, and sometimes Temperance might be heard also, in a more subdued key, grumbling out some unattractive refrain of an air she did not know very well. Out-of-doors the apple-picking had begun. The farmer had always looked forward to Jim Fales's superior usefulness at this season. Jim was at this moment near the top of the high fall-sweeting tree, and, apparently impatient with his charge of hand-picking the fruit, shuffled it into his basket with all the haste possible. As he pushed his way, head and shoulders, through the topmost branches, his eyes beheld Mr. Dale at the spinning-room window, near by, and the friends exchanged as cordial and ceremonious greetings as if they had not parted from each other at the breakfast table three quarters of an hour before.

"See here," said Jim confidentially, after having carefully surveyed the world beneath him, "was it you was talking to Doris, as I come in the yard last night?"

"No," said Richard Dale gravely. "No, it was not I," he repeated, gazing with much interest at his questioner's countenance, which suddenly looked like a clock-face that has lost its hands.

"I thought I'd ask. I had some misgivin's before the words had left my mouth," the youth explained, and all at once drew back within the green boughs, and was lost to sight. Presently, with much difficulty, he transferred the clumsy ladder to a tree still closer to the window, and climbed it with an empty basket, as if the path of duty led that way, and no other. Dick was inclined to resent this; the brilliant color of the fruit had delighted his eyes, and there was little of it left, at any rate. He felt a sudden pang as Jim rustled about among the leaves, and hated him as he selected a fair apple and began to devour it with evident satisfaction. "I think there ain't no such cripsy ones on the place as them," he announced. "Have one?" and he twisted another from the tree, and gave it a leisurely toss at the window, where Dick barely succeeded in catching it. The invasion of his favorite outlook made him impatient. He put the apple on the window-sill, and took up his book again, as if he did not mean to be interrupted. This harvesting hinted at the spoiling of his beloved surroundings. Somehow, there had been so slight and amiable a change in the landscape and the weather itself, that Dick had not been led to think of an end of his pleasant arrangements and his sunshine holiday. He sighed, as if he were obliged to go back to a veritable treadmill, and presently looked out of the window again. The green old apple-tree, with its flecks of red fruit, had been a very lovely thing to look at against the blue and white September skies, and when he first discovered the spinning-room the apples were little more than half grown.

Jim had been on the alert to catch the least sign of renewed attention, and said softly, leaning toward his listener, "I had it right over about seeing you an' Doris out in the boat yisterday forenoon. Dan Lester must have been fit to swear. He can't abide that anybody should look at Doris but him. We roughed him fearful one day down on the ma'sh, when we was getting the salt hay in."

"He's a good fellow, isn't he?" asked Dale, as carelessly as possible.

"First-rate," replied Jim, with another survey of the immediate neighborhood. "Folks has wondered a good deal that him an' Doris is so slow about gettin' things settled; but land! folks must have something to work over in their minds. I don't expect she sets half so much by him as he does by her, any way," he added confidentially. Jim Fales admired the new resident of the Marsh Island with all his heart. Dale had been very friendly with the young fellow, and seemed, to one person at least, quite the hero; but now he felt that there was danger of disloyalty if this conversation were allowed to go on. His desire to hear all that Jim was more than ready to say was promptly quenched, as he gave a careless nod to the Romeo at his balcony, and retreated to the opposite side of the room. He had been told nothing yet that he was sur-

prised to hear, but an undefined dread arose
lest there should be some evident recognition
of his own personal interest in the tale.

Somehow, Dick was not inclined toward
painting; his interest in that once-absorbing
avocation had been dwindling, of late. No
wonder; he had never done so many good
bits in the same length of time before. The
sketch of Doris did not seem so necessary
and inevitable as it had once, for Doris herself claimed the better part of his thoughts.
Doris as she had looked at him yesterday
under the great beech-tree was never to be
forgotten, and a strange thrill went over
him at the remembrance. She was very
sweet and silent and busy that morning,
and the temptation came to him to win this
little kingdom of the world and the glory of
it. He must take Doris away from her own
world, — that would be the trouble; he certainly was possessed of no gifts or qualifications for tilling the soil. He smiled as he
whispered to himself,

"His highest plot
To plant the bergamot,"

and wondered if, with all his experience and
a half weariness and impatience of the fashionable world, he should make the worst sort

of country gentleman. His imagination flew quickly about the old farm. Delightful as it was, it might be made infinitely more attractive. Dick almost loved Doris's father, but he was not so pleased with the thought of her mother, though this was followed with a quick self-reproach. He could not disguise the fact that there was a tinge of unreality over all these uncharacteristic visions of himself. He must go away soon, and leave Doris to her true lover. She had looked very troubled once or twice that day. After all, he did not believe in making himself miserable; but at that moment the thought of Dan Lester's triumph made Dick amazingly angry. Why should such a beautiful creature as Doris be degraded into an ordinary country housekeeper, and lose the better sort of love and favor and true knowledge of life? It must not be; the young man's heart beat fast with a new inspiration. If Doris loved him and he loved her, they would face the future together, and his face grew pale as he stood still in the little studio, looking straight forward, but seeing nothing for a moment; then the radiant bubble had burst, and all that was left was the same uncertainty and vexation of spirit as before.

"James," old Mr. Owen was saying under the window, " I thought you had better pick those fall-sweetings first."

" They was covered with dew, sir," responded the defendant. " There ain't but a few of these, and then I'm going back to finish. The sun strikes here earlier," and Jim began a self-satisfied whistling, as he let a slender, unburdened branch rustle back into place.

Dick spent a miserable, wandering day. He felt unpardonably thrown off his track, and as if he must not allow such weakness and foolishness. He might have made a fool of himself on a good many occasions, but, thank Heaven, he had always behaved like a man, and not, as now, like a silly woman. It was difficult even to announce his determination to go back to town the next week, and this distressed knight strayed about the familiar places of the farm as if he were bidding them farewell. It was an afternoon to be laughed at heartily some day, — he knew himself well enough to be sure of that; but a sigh followed this reflection, which was more than likely to be repeated.

XVII.

Later in the day Dick came through the clock-room, and stopped a moment to look for a book. There was a noise of strange voices outside, and just as he reached the outer door some one knocked hurriedly, — a fumbling, unaccustomed sort of knock. It must be confessed that he recognized with something like a shock the familiar figure on the broad doorstep.

"For pity's sake, Richard, how came you here?" exclaimed this unexpected guest, forgetting for the moment her evidently exciting errand, as she gazed at her nephew in complete astonishment. "I believe I never was so thankful to see you," she went on, without waiting for any explanation. "We have lost our way, though I was sure that I knew the right turn. You see this is a new coachman" (tone nearly inaudible, but more spirited). "Johnson became so unreliable that I had to dismiss him, after fourteen years' service. I believe we have broken the bolts of the victoria " (louder), " and I was really in despair; I have already walked quite a long distance. Do find somebody to look at the carriage and see if it will be safe to drive home; we have promised to dine with the Chaunceys this evening. You surely remember Mrs. Farley? — May I present my nephew, Mr. Dale? I have n't the slightest idea how he happens to be here, but I really never was so glad to see him in my life."

The very buttons of the new coachman's new coat were surprising to Mr. Richard Dale, but to such emergencies as this he was more than equal. He bowed smilingly to Mrs. Farley, and helped her to alight, and then inspected the damaged vehicle under the guidance of Johnson's successor. "That's a very simple affair," this useful nephew said, with charming reassurance. " Mr. Owen is sure to be able to put it right in a few minutes. You must go into the house and rest yourselves, and I will take the carriage up the yard."

" He seems entirely at home," meditated Mrs. Winchester, as she gave a sigh of relief and turned toward her friend. Mrs. Farley had become somewhat impatient with the needless excitement and fears of her companion, who had been behaving as if they were wrecked among cannibals. She had known real disasters herself, but Mrs. Winchester was so used to a luxurious routine of life that she was quite helpless in anything that approached the nature of an accident. She was accustomed to the opportune appearance of her gentlemen friends, and it was only a repetition of the usual state of affairs that Dick should open the farmhouse door for her when she was overwhelmed with anxiety at finding herself belated on a strange road, a dozen miles from home.

"I could have made the carriage all right, sir," said the distressed servant, as soon as they were out of the ladies' hearing. He evidently thought it best to forestall reproach for his want of resource. "Mrs. Winchester kept telling me the roads, though I knew we were all the time getting too far from home, please, sir. And she screeched with fright when I was getting down from the box. I had a bit of stout cord, too. I am with her only a month, sir, or I'd know every road within reach."

Dick nodded indulgently, and the new retainer held himself in his most upright and stiffly effective position as they approached hospitable Mr. Owen, who was quite unconscious of the town-like splendor of this appearance; and wondering Jim Fales, who was nearly overcome with awe and delight.

As for Mrs. Owen, she had promptly come forward to welcome the strangers, after first having watched them through the kitchen blinds, with a temporary loss of self-confidence. The ladies were much pleased with the simple hospitality and friendliness of her greeting, and presently were invited to leave the sitting-room, where they had established themselves, and accompany their hostess to the best parlor. They had been delighted with the clock-room; but the parlor, which had been refurnished by good Mrs. Owen according to her own mistaken lights, had always been shunned by Dick with ill-concealed abhorrence, and was now more than ever damp and close, and pervaded with the odor of its woolen carpet and haircloth upholstery. The blinds were opened, and the fading light of day entered somewhat doubtfully. Mrs. Winchester grew more and more puzzled. What could Dick mean by being here, evidently quite familiar with the household, and never letting her know of his whereabouts?

There was a light step in the hall outside; somebody pushed back a chair which had been moved out of its place; then a young woman stood, surprised, at the best room door.

Mrs. Farley, who was ready at conversation, and a most sympathetic soul, had been describing their wanderings and distress to her new acquaintance. Now she noticed a new look of interest in her auditor's pleasant face, and Mrs. Owen, without waiting for a pause in the narrative, said, with motherly pride, "Come in, Doris, do. This is Mr. Dale's aunt, and — I did n't catch the other lady's name? They met with an accident, and lost their way besides. Yes, I 'm sure it was confusing," she added encouragingly to Mrs. Farley, who showed no desire to continue, and just then met Mrs. Winchester's confidential and most meaning glance and gesture with an amused smile.

Doris hesitated on the threshold; she was never awkward, but who would not have quailed now? She had not heard the visitors enter, but the next instant she had taken her place beside them, and was even busy with thought for their comfort. The place displeased her strangely; these guests dismayed her. " Would n't you like to go up to the room Mr. Dale has used for his studio?" she asked, with sudden self-reliance. " I am sure he will want to show you his pictures."

The ladies rose with alacrity; and presently Dick turned from a consultation with Mr. Owen and the coachman to see them coming up the yard. " That was very clever of Doris," he said to himself gratefully, and nodded to them as they disappeared. Mrs. Owen was of the party, and almost directly the delinquent nephew's ears caught the sound of delighted exclamations. Then he saw Doris come down the steep outer stairway of the spinning-room, looking preoccupied, and go quickly by, stopping to confer with Temperance, whose head emerged from one of the kitchen windows.

In a few minutes he saw the fair daughter of the house returning with a white-covered tray of fruit and cakes. These dear, good people ! this lovely Doris! He was glad enough when his part of the work was done, and he could join the pleased and pacified company.

"This is very kind of you, to make my shipwrecked friends so comfortable, Mrs. Owen," he said. Dick's aunt thought he had never been so handsome. Doris looked at him, and felt as if he were again a stranger. She had needed only this hint and visible evidence of his previous life and associations to disengage herself, as it were, from a sense of entire familiarity.

"You will have the moon to light you home, if you wait," Dick was saying. "I do not think that you need hurry away. I have told the coachman a much shorter road back. He seems an excellent fellow. I wonder that you risked your life so long with Johnson."

"You should have followed the short road yourself long ago, Dick," said Mrs. Winchester. "But I will not scold you, after seeing these sketches. You never began to do anything so charming. I dare say that I am quite faithless about the new man," she went on, "but since I have found you I mean to lay claim to you. We cannot possibly get home before evening: the horses are very slow; you know that you always make fun of them. Dick, you really must go back with us, and I will send you over as early as you like in the morning."

There was no mistaking the sincerity and insistence of Mrs. Winchester's plea, and her nephew consented, though without enthusiasm. Perhaps it was just as well, after all, and a little later he found himself spinning along the East Road on the box of the victoria. The maligned horses were much excited at their unusual delay, and more than anxious for their supper. Mrs. Winchester's thoughts were busy now with hopes of reaching home in time for her evening engagement, all other perplexities having been dispersed.

"Do you think they would let me have butter, another year?" she asked once, with sudden eagerness; but Dick was sure that he did not know, and she concluded, from his evident lack of interest, that the butter might not be entirely to his taste. "I dare say they would not care to bring it so far," Mrs. Winchester announced magnanimously. In spite of the sketches, she could not help thinking that the young girl's undeniable good looks had something to do with Dick's going into retreat in such a determined fashion.

The western sky was clear and shining after the sunset, and there was already a glow of coming moonlight in the east as the belated victoria trundled homeward. The lamps were lit in one wayside farmhouse after another, the shadows were gathering faster and faster in the fields, and some tracts of woodland were dark as night and cold as late October when they drove under the overarching boughs. The two ladies were very warm and comfortable in their wraps; they leaned back against their cushions, and talked together in low voices about the house and the people they had just left. They were pleased with their adventure, now that all danger was past, and it seemed a great joke that Dick should have been discovered and drawn from his hiding-place. Mrs. Farley kindly took the young man's part, and spoke of his work with admiration, but his aunt amused herself with little jokes at his expense; therefore Dick himself was conscious of a great liking for Mrs. Farley, who was an old friend of his mother's, and had lived in China for many years. Dick assured himself, with sudden satisfaction, that it would not be such a bad thing to go to the East Indies. Bradish and he had often talked about it. Nothing could give Bradish a better chance; it was exactly in his line.

Mrs. Winchester, after a long pause, repeated an accusation about Dick's love for peaches. He had stolen some once which had been procured at vast expense for a dinner party, and he was an altogether unamiable nephew as he turned half-way round to wave a deprecatory hand at his accuser. Aunt Susan was a kind-hearted creature, and was considered very clever by her friends. Dick was obliged to confess that he had heard her talk charmingly to other people; but somehow she usually treated him like a school-boy, and they were not apt to enjoy each other. Why need she hunt up all those silly old stories of his infancy every time they found themselves together? He wrapped the thin lap-rug about his knees, and settled himself into his place, as if he did not wish to be spoken to again. It was strange how entirely out of sympathy he was with this change of scene.

The victoria was driven into its own avenue, after a while. The lights were bright in the great house, and the alarmed maids came hurrying out to hear what had happened. Dick was recognized with surprise, and as the coachman turned the horses away from the door one or two comrades appeared from behind the hedge, and walked beside him, asking eager questions.

"We lost our way, — that was all," said the mistress, in an amiable, clear voice, to the little audience. "Luckily we found Mr. Dale, who has been sketching, and he brought us home. We must have some tea up-stairs directly, and Mr. Dale will have supper presently in the dining-room. Dear me, how late we shall be!" and Mrs. Winchester and her guest quickly ascended the long staircase. It seemed a pity that their allegiance to society did not permit any comfort or rest at that moment. A great fire was leaping and crackling in the wide hall fireplace, and the chairs near by looked most inviting. Dick chose the largest, and pulled it close to the hearth; he heard a scurrying to and fro up-stairs, the doors were opened and shut many times, and his aunt once recalled a loitering maid impatiently to add further directions about his own supper. She had been annoyed because he had disobeyed her command to bring his evening clothes, and had reprimanded him sharply as they were driving homeward. "I am not in any mood for squiring to-night," he told himself, and smiled to think what joy they would have presently in relating their adventure to their friends.

The ladies came rustling down; the cocoons of the victoria were transformed into moth-like creatures of sober splendors and soft raiment. Here and there they glittered and shone, and Dick examined them with sudden interest. There was a thinness and poverty about the dress of those women at the farm, compared with this richness and stateliness. Doris Owen would be beautiful in such quiet tints; the simplicity of true elegance would suit her exactly.

"I am admiring you both immensely," the young man said. "I have been quite unused to such magnificence, you know."

"How charming it was at the farm!" and Mrs. Farley smiled at him in a most sympathetic fashion. "I shall so often remember the spinning-room and the clock-room, and all the rest of it. What a pretty idea to make that your studio! But you ought to have kept the spinning-wheels, and asked the rustic maidens to come and whir them while you painted."

"I am certain that the peaches won the day," interrupted Mrs. Winchester, with conscious unconsciousness and a good deal of emphasis. "It was all very picturesque, but I can't imagine your being contented there for a month or more, unless you happened to see your favorite fruit in a green state, and determined to wait and enjoy it. But I am heartily pleased about the sketches. I can see every one now! I can't forgive myself for leaving that delightful bit where the two little white sails are following each other through the green marsh. I dare say you will throw it away upon one of your cronies, when you go back to town."

"It shall be yours from this moment," Dick responded gallantly, while they made little bows at each other. The aunt was very fond of him; and indeed he returned her unselfish affection, after his own fashion.

The ladies deplored the impossibility of staying at home, and waited impatiently for things they had forgotten; finally they went out into the moonlight. "I should never think of going at this late hour," said the hostess, "but they will be so anxious to know what has become of us. I have a feeling that we shall make ourselves very interesting, my dear. They would be disappointed not to see you!"

Mrs. Farley gave her shoulders a little shrug. She did not think these neighbors very amusing, and she was curious to know more about Mr. Dick Dale. She wished that she had ventured to act her own pleasure, and send a regret to her entertainers.

As for Dick, his ears had caught the sound of the sea, as he stood in the doorway watching the ladies drive away. He lighted a cigar, and went across the grounds to a small summer-house, which looked ghostly and felt damp; and here he sat at the edge of the high cliff, and saw the familiar country, sea and shore. The moon was high in the sky; could it be possible that he saw it only last night as it rose above the marshes? That seemed like a year ago. The small fire of the cigar went out, and the world instantly grew large and exceedingly cold; then Dick gave a great shiver, and went back to the house. The servant who met him looked displeased; they had been looking for him everywhere, and his supper was waiting. He had seldom enjoyed a supper more than he did this, but once or twice he looked up, and was obliged to recognize the fact that he had expected to see Doris opposite him, as usual. In the morning he would ask his aunt's advice upon the subject of a proper gift for Mrs. Owen. But that night he made a selection of new books, and marched up to his own room in excellent season. He well knew his aunt's love for a bit of midnight gossip, and he was not sure of his answers for some simple questions which she would be sure to ask. He wondered what was going on at the farmhouse; his thoughts kept flying in that direction, and this once familiar life became a little strange and constraining.

As he might have known, the Owens were taking great pleasure in talking over the surprising events of the afternoon. Doris alone had not much to say. Temperance was considerably displeased because one of the guests had offered her money, just as they were ready to begin their homeward drive. She had refused it indignantly, with the information that she had done nothing to earn it, and a wise suspicion of such unnecessary patronage.

"I suppose that was her way of showing gratitude," said Doris, with a sigh. "I dare say such people find enough who are ready to take pay for everything. They were very pleasant, I 'm sure."

The farmer looked at his daughter, as he sat reading close by the lamp. This was the day for the Semi-Weekly Tribune, and he was deeply interested in a political argument, but he did not go on with it directly. Doris was very pale to-night. Something had evidently gone wrong with her, and he accused himself of being neglectful and thoughtless. They had not been so much together as usual this fall. Doris was grown into a woman now. The truth flashed upon him that she was no longer the childish creature he had loved and fondly wished to keep beside him. Dan Lester had behaved strangely, but he was a high-strung fellow, and might have had some foolish notions about young Dale. He would stop and have a word with Dan to-morrow, when he must go through Sussex. Perhaps he would take Doris herself along, and this thought gave Israel Owen great pleasure. Dan was the best fellow in the world, and seemed like a son already. There was no need for his tinkering away at a trade, if he and the little girl made it up. Dan had uncommon good sense about farming, and he should have his way, — he should have his way. A sudden remembrance of the little flag came to the farmer's mind. The colors of it were faded now: May was long ago. The family never had gathered round the evening light, in all these years, that the father had not sadly, and as if for the first time, missed his son. To-night they had established themselves in the wide kitchen, after supper was over; the clock-room was a trifle damp, and for some reason or other a little cheerless.

Mrs. Owen was still revolving the news of Dan Lester's good fortune in her mind, and viewing it in all aspects. She had been longing to ask Temperance certain questions, and she wondered if Dan himself had said anything to Doris the evening before; but she was not yet ready to throw her long-cherished opposition and objection to the four winds. As if she were afraid of being even suspected of these thoughts, she hastened to talk about the afternoon's guests again. "I'm real glad it was so that they saw the parlor," she said once, in a gratified tone.

XVIII.

Mr. Dale was just reflecting that he should soon be very sleepy indeed, and that he had not been awake so late for several weeks, when a sound was heard outside his door, followed by a light knocking.

"Come in!" he said reluctantly, and then almost laughed aloud at the innocence and good-nature of his aunt's expression. "I might have known she would not let me off so easily," he said to himself, and rose from his comfortable arm-chair without a word, as Mrs. Winchester entered, though he looked as if he were ready to be informed of so unseasonable an errand.

"I knew that you could n't be asleep," declared Mrs. Winchester, resuming her beaming expression, which had been abandoned temporarily, at the sight of the flaring candles. Dick really was as much care as when he was ten years old and her orphan ward. "I thought you must be reading when I saw the bright light, as I came up the avenue. The Chaunceys were really quite hurt because you did n't make your appearance. Dinner was later than usual, — at any rate, only the soup had been served; and Will Chauncey was detained in town, so that there was an empty seat for you next Kate Dent. She is here for a week it seems. I always thought her extremely handsome and attractive. You have n't seen her since she returned from abroad have you?"

"I believe not," answered Dick patiently.

"I see that you have the Village on the Cliff. Was there ever anything so charming and full of color!" pursued the little lady, after a short pause. She was comfortably settled in a low chair, and was taking a careful survey of her nephew. Really, his clothes were much the worse for wear; he looked not unlike a farmer, himself. "I have been telling everybody what a lovely face that old Mr. Owen has," she continued enthusiastically. "I wish you were fond of figure-sketching. I should like a portrait of him immensely; just a suggestion of all but his eyes, you know, — in charcoal, perhaps."

"All but his eyes," repeated Dick cynically. "I think" —

"Oh, you know what I mean," she laughed. "Don't be superior, Dick, if you have such a misfortune as a stupid old aunt. I meant, of course, that his eyes are so fine I cared most for that part of his likeness. He has such a pathetic expression at times. A most sincere, kindly old man. He seems very fond of you. What did he mean by telling me that you bore a welcome resemblance?"

"He thought, when I first went there, that I was like his only son, who was killed in the war," answered Dick, in a more sympathetic tone than he had used before. "I supposed he had forgotten about that."

"And the old handmaiden, too. Charity did they call her? No, Temperance! She has an interesting, blighted sort of face. She was very indignant because I offered her some money. I suppose it was rude of me, but one gets so used to that way of expressing gratitude in this mercenary world."

"You must wait until you die to pay your debts to your friends gracefully," announced the host of the occasion, beginning to pace up and down the room. It was a familiar sign of his impatience, but Mrs. Winchester did not mean to be dismissed so soon.

"I never thought of that," she said, apparently much pleased. "Yes, we can give money to whom we like, — it is the way we do the thing;" whereupon Dick came and stood before his aunt, and regarded her benignantly.

"Do scold me," he said. "I know you are tired to death, aunt Susy, but you must do your duty by me before you sleep. I must be off early to-morrow. I have set my heart upon making a few sketches over at Sussex."

"I have always wished that somebody would do that very thing. To me it is the most charmingly picturesque little place. But, Richard, you must surely give me a few days before I go back to town; you used to like to stay with me. And this year, of all others, while Nelly and the children are away, and I have missed them so much, I do think you should not have forgotten me."

"You always have such a houseful of people," grumbled Dick. "Yes, I suppose I can come for next week; or you may put me down for all next summer, if you like that better. Don't be foolish, aunt Susan. You always have laughed at me, but you never must let me make you sorry," and he laid his hand gently on her little lace cap and soft gray hair, and then turned away quickly, and walked over to the window. " What bright moonlight ! " he said. " Do go to bed, aunt. Be friendly, and take yourself off now. You have no idea how early I had my breakfast."

"Dick," said the little woman, raising herself to her full height and coming to stand before him, — " Dick, my dear, I begin to think you had better let me have your traps brought here to-morrow or next day. I don't quite like your staying there any more. They 're good people and ever so fond of you ; but for their sakes, and that nice girl's sake especially, I hate to have you run into any sort of danger. I think it has been a great thing for you in many ways, and a charming experience on the whole ; but believe me, you had better come away. I really should be hurt if you did n't come to me, now that I have told the Chaunceys that you have been hiding yourself so near me for weeks and weeks. If you were a girl yourself, I should feel differently ; but with your good looks and your fortune, and your way of making everybody like you, I think it is all a great risk."

Dick tried to laugh at this determined charge, but at that moment he felt as a girl might truly feel, not like a man. "I am all right, thank you, dear old lady," he said. "Doris has a lover already, if that is what you mean. Perhaps you think that Temperance is setting her nets."

"Good old soul!" responded Mrs. Winchester, with some spirit. "I won't have you make such low jokes, Dick."

"I like her, myself," answered the young man, angrily. "I like every one of them at the island. If I ever amount to anything, I shall thank those sincere, simple people for setting me the example of following my duty and working hard and steadily. I wish sometimes that I had n't two cents in the world. I never was so happy in my life as I have been there; nobody ever asked whether I was rich or poor. You have to be put into an honest place like that to know anything of yourself. You can't think how tired and sick I am of the kind of life I have somehow drifted into."

"I have always felt that you were capable of better things," agreed aunt Susan, much moved by the gloomy eagerness of her nephew. "But now that you have had your lesson you must profit by it; you would waste yourself even more if you stayed long on that farm. Think of your opportunities! I dare say you have found time for thought, and I congratulate you; but what are you going to do with your new energy? Dick, dear, I have been a sort of mother to you. I have loved you, and tried to make up for the loss of your own mother. Now don't be foolish and sentimental, and fall in love with that pretty girl. You 're spasmodic; you 're led by your enthusiasms. I think she is really charming to look at, but she is not a fit wife for you."

"Aunt Susan," and the listener to these exhortations faced about suddenly from the window, "Doris Owen is the most beautiful woman I ever knew. She 's capable of anything. She is not inferior. She may lack certain experiences, but she is equal to meeting them. She is a fit wife for any man."

"Oh dear, dear!" groaned aunt Susan at this incomprehensible nephew, "is it as bad as that?"

"Bad as what?" said Dick, ready to fight for his rights. "Come, this is too late a council; we never should have fallen to discussing such things by daylight."

"You must tell me all about it. How far have you really gone?" persisted the troubled woman.

"Gone?" exclaimed Dick Dale. "I have done nothing at all. If you wish to know whether I have asked Doris Owen to be my wife, I certainly have not. And nobody but you should drive me to the wall in this fashion, and question me as if I were a schoolboy."

Mrs. Winchester asks to be forgiven. She trusts Dick, and tells him so. She has never been ashamed of him yet. All these things she says in a matter-of-fact tone, and then bids him good-night, and goes away. Dick does not kiss her, after his old fashion, though she wishes he would, as she lets go his strong hand and looks at him an instant before she flits away from the door, stepping softly along the hall in her light little shoes. A moment after it is too late, Dick is sorry he did not give her the kiss, and then he considers the propriety of his last statement. He liked, after all, to be treated in exactly this way; it was the only bit of home life that seemed to be always his own. He was invariably called to account by his aunt Susan, and as a general thing took his catechising meekly, as became the nephew whom a kind fate had put under Mrs. Winchester's charge through his early years. The time of boyish marauding, of shirking lessons and abusing clothes and tormenting servants, was happily over with, but his misdemeanors were only transferred to more dangerous quarters. Poor Dick! he felt very young and very willful now; it was only city life and association that made him look upon himself as the Methuselah of society.

The sea was dashing against the low cliffs, not far away. He listened to the sound of it until he fell asleep. The waves were calling and waiting, and calling again, louder than before. The great sea was farther away from the Marsh Island, and there the cry of it seemed more distant and dull; here there was an insistence, a mercilessness, in its voice. There was a great pain in such a consciousness of great possibilities and miserable achievements. Was Mrs. Winchester wrong or right? Her horizons might indeed be contracted, but her directions were as true as the compass.

XIX.

EARLY the next morning Doris and her father set forth on their long drive to the outer shore. It would have been hard to say which of them was most pleased with the prospect of this expedition. Doris had looked unwontedly gratified, and even relieved, when she accepted the invitation, as they sat together at breakfast, and indeed was ready some time before there was any need of it, and stood waiting in the yard with almost childish impatience. Israel Owen was in a most placid and serene mood, but tried to take the unusual pleasure as indifferently as possible, and consulted his wife with gratifying deference as to the best bargain that might be made for some hay. He was going to hold a solemn business conference with the overseer and manager of a large estate on the neighboring sea-coast.

Mrs. Owen was mildly excited, and called loudly after her husband, when he was fairly out of the yard, not to make an out-and-out present of his hay-mow to those who would never thank him for it; then she returned to the kitchen, and became stolid and silent. Temperance Kipp was also silent for a time, but increasingly energetic, and kept hurrying from room to room, driving before her an alarmed flock of resourceless flies. She complained of this unseasonable escort, and bewailed the fact once or twice that when fall flies hived into the house in that fashion they were always a sign of changing weather. "I urged the 'Square not to ride way over there in the open wagon," she mentioned reproachfully, " and all he had to say was that he wanted the sun on him. I hope 't won't come on a cold rain this afternoon." But the mistress of the house preserved a scornful indifference, as if she had resolved never to make another futile protest against waywardness and folly.

There was a great deal to be done that day, but neither of the elder women had offered the slightest opposition to Doris's taking a holiday, or seemed offended by her absence. Indeed, it was an evident relief for the time being, and the current of affairs presently flowed with its usual tranquillity. Temperance would have liked to put more of her thoughts into speech, but Martha Owen judiciously continued to hold her peace and conceal whatever excitement she may have felt.

"Seems to me it feels like old times," Temperance ventured, as she bent over the ironing-board. "There, I should really miss doin' up Mr. Dale's shirts, if he was to go away. They do polish so handsome. This one's a-beginnin' to crack out a little. Everything he buys is good quality, and it's the best economy, certain. I wonder if he's goin' to get back before afternoon?"

Meanwhile, Doris was growing more and more pleased with the day's enterprise. To be sure, there were clouds in the sky, but they afforded a subject for discussion rather than alarm, and the weather suited exactly. The young girl looked pale at first, but the light wind and warm sunshine soon brought a flicker of bright color into her cheeks, where her father quickly saw it and rejoiced. "They've tormented her about to pieces, amongst them," he assured himself, and struck at a bee, which had alighted on the horse's neck, with his clumsy, long-lashed whip. "Let them work, I say. Young folks will be young folks;" and presently, where the Sussex road branched off, he determinedly passed it by, though the other highway made their journey two or three miles longer. "I thought I'd just look in to see how Asher's folks are gettin' on," he explained. " We might as well make a good day of it, and go one road and come the other. Don't you say so, Doris?"

Doris smiled assent. " What a long while it is since we have been over this way, father!" she said.

"The country does look handsome, for the time of the year," the farmer announced. " I believe I feel just like having a play-time myself. It makes me think of when you used to go ridin' about with me, when you were a little girl. I recollect one time I thought I couldn't get along without you. Why, you used to want to be set up on the horse's back and ride forwards an' back in the furrows, when I was ploughing; and one spell you used to get right on to the plough, and roll off sometimes, too," and they both laughed at this reminiscence.

Doris remembered that she had been with her father less than usual the last few months, and felt very sorry. She would not forget his pleasure in that way again. He must have missed her more than she had suspected; but he was in unusually good spirits that morning.

"Seems to me you're dressed up pretty smart to go travelin' with a rusty old farmer like me. I believe I should ha' put on my best co't," said Israel; and they laughed together again, and looked at one another affectionately.

"I like you best as you are," the girl answered shyly. "I should think we felt strange:" but she did not meet her father's eyes again; they were both too conscious of each other's thought.

Many a man and woman gave the travelers a pleasant greeting, as they jogged along. They stopped before other doors than Asher's, and told the news and heard it with equal satisfaction. One observant neighbor took a shrewd look at Doris, and gave an opinion that she was looking a little peaked; at which Mr. Owen was startled, and stole a glance at his daughter, who eagerly insisted that she was very well. The father had a somewhat uncanny gift for understanding secrets that were not told him; especially those concealed with the care which is complete betrayal to such intuition. He seemed possessed to-day by an unusual spirit of observation, and presently, after neither had spoken for a few minutes, Doris found him directing significant glances at her hands, which were clasped together, holding the pair of unused gloves which her mother had suggested at the last moment before they left home.

"Seems to me some o' the rest of 'em might do the apple-parin'," he said, half to himself. "You'll spile your pretty fingers, Doris."

"Why, father!" exclaimed the girl, appealingly; and Israel Owen was much disturbed by the alarm and surprised awakening of her tone.

"'T wa'n't wise," he reflected, and struck at the horse's ear again. "I don't know what my wits are about to-day;" and then he laughed aloud, as unconcernedly as possible, and said, "Blamed if I don't hit him next time!" as if the eluding bee were really his chief object of thought. The father and daughter had been seldom troubled by such self-consciousness. The even flow of their home-life had lately been fretted by unaccustomed currents, and it was impossible to keep a straight course. But Doris smiled when the whip-lash proved itself invincible, and the horse, bewildered by such unusual strokes, darted along the road. The bee had done old Major no harm by lighting so persistently on his already thickened coat, but its presence served the driver an excellent turn.

"I declare, I do feel glad to be out-of-door to-day," said the farmer, quite himself again. "I've been under cover seeing to the fruit, and so on, and I begun to feel sort of hustled. You brought along something besides this little cape o' yourn, did n't you, sister? We 're likely to have it cooler down to the shore. I declare, this is a sightly place!" and he stopped the horse at the top of a hill, under a great maple-tree, while a flock of the early fallen leaves came racing toward them along the ground, like a crowd of children at play. "There, you get a plain view here, if you do anywhere; the country lays itself out like a map. See the shipping down Westmarket way. The masts are in thick as bean-poles, all ready to take a lot of poor fellows out an' sink 'em," the old landsman grumbled, as he looked toward the white town clustered about a distant harbor side.

"I always seem to forget what a little ways it is from home right across. It can't be half so far as it is by the nearest road," said Doris, as they went on again. "See, father, you get across our marsh, and then row over to the great white beach, and cross the sand heaps to the back river and go up over the quarry hills, and right down into Westmarket!"

"I have followed that road many a time, when I was younger," answered Mr. Owen, turning to look back at the lowlands. "I used to think 't was a good deal farther than need be, too, when I was travelin' back and forwards from the harbor, courtin' your mother. The folks at home thought I was n't old enough to know my own mind, and did n't favor us no great;" and Israel Owen smiled with an unforgotten sense of triumph, while Doris grew sober again. It had been very comfortable to forget herself for a few minutes.

"Somehow, everything looks pleasant to-day," she said. "Perhaps you'll get through in time to go to Westmarket. I want to do some shopping, and mother always likes to hear from there."

"The days are n't so long as they have been," said the farmer sagely. "We'll see what we can do, Doris," and presently they were in the lower country again.

It was a famous day for crows: from one field after another a flight of them took heavily to their wings, and, as if unwillingly, mounted to the higher air. They cawed loudly, and appeared to have business of a public nature on hand. Some were migrating, and others were contemptuously rebuking these wanderers, and making their arrangements to winter in their familiar woods: it was all a great chatter and clatter and commotion. The affairs of human beings were but trivial in comparison. Helpless creatures, who crept to and fro on the face of the earth, and were drawn about by captive animals of lesser intellect, were not worth noticing, and the great black birds sailed magnificently down the sky, with the fresh breeze cool in their beaks and the sunlight shining on their sombre wings. Whatever might be said of their morals, they were masters of the air, and could fly, while men could not. Doris watched them with childlike pleasure, perhaps with a faint instinctive recognition of the ancient auspices; the home people had always laughed at her fancy for the crows ever since she could remember.

The end of the journey was reached; the business talk was promptly begun, and, finding that the owners of the great house had gone away to town, Doris left the wagon, and went strolling toward the shore. The noise of the sea sounded louder and nearer than usual, as if a storm were coming or the tide just turning; the gray snow-birds were fluttering and calling one another in the thickets, as she went by. It was not the first time that she had driven to this place with her father. He had sold hay here for many years, and the Marsh Island was one of the reservoirs upon which the luxurious housekeeping depended for its supplies. The people themselves sometimes came over to the farm, and there was a pleasant bond of interest and respect between the two families. Mrs. Owen had fretted and planned about Doris's appearance, but the girl herself was glad when she saw the great house deserted and in winter order, though she looked at it with a new curiosity and eagerness which she could hardly have explained.

The horse had been fastened and the two men had disappeared before Doris was fairly across the lawn, and she was glad enough. She liked the freedom of her solitary ramble, and presently went round to the side of the house next the sea, and seated herself on the broad balustrade, among the frost-bitten vines that had shaded and adorned the wide piazza all summer. Below, on a terrace, the hardier flowers were still blooming, and she wondered that any home could seem more enticing than this. It had almost an appealing look to her, with its deserted garden and so noble an outlook and surrounding. She never had felt so close a sympathy with this more involved and complex mode of existence. This all belonged in a way to Mr. Dale, and was familiar to him; it was the sort of life he had always lived, and she was familiar with Mr. Dale.

A quick flush showed itself for a moment on her cheek, as she spoke his name in her thoughts. She looked along the house front, and rose to peep wistfully in at the heart-shaped hole of the nearest window shutter; but this was not the most satisfactory thing in the world, and she turned to break a blossoming tendril of the late morning-glories that had sheltered themselves under the cornice. Then she went down the steps that were littered with fallen leaves, and along the path that led to the cliffs and the sea. The great hemlocks and pines had conquered their territory, and stood strong and vigorous among the ledges; the barberry bushes were bright with fruit, and the song-sparrows played at summer sports and kept a famous holiday. Doris stopped in the tennis court to hear them sing, and looked round delightedly at the quaint place, with its high walls of the rough stone of the hill on three sides, and the fading hollyhocks that had stood discreetly back out of the way of the players all summer. The grass was smooth and as green as ever; a tall poplar that stood on the ledge above had been dropping down some of its yellow leaves, and the warm sunshine was filling every corner of the windless pleasure-ground. Nothing had ever spoken so plainly to this girl of the pursuit of amusement which belongs to many lives. She thought with almost contempt of the idle ways of rich people, having been brought face to face with a sterner fashion of things; and then a more generous sense of the added care and responsibility of such householding as this made her go on her way bewildered and yet contented. Just beyond Doris found a seat for herself on the brown pine needles, beside a great green juniper, where she could look down over the rocks and see the white waves come tumbling in from the open sea. One might say of her that she had been confronted with a materialization of her vague ambitions and hopes, and that these shapes of luxury and worldly consequence were by no means without power. The crows kept up a desperate argument with each other overhead, and for the first time in her life Doris thought them too clamorous and obtrusive, as they balanced themselves clumsily on the high branches of the pine-trees. What should she do, — or rather, what was going to be done with her? Her life was not familiar and easily lived any more, poor Doris! She shrank from the great blue sea as if it were her own future of surprise and uncertainty; the friendly country-side of her childhood all lay behind her. She felt as if she were on the verge of a greater sea, which might prove either wonderful happiness or bitter misery; and confused and dismayed by her loyalty to both her lovers, she hid her face in her hands. If she only knew what to do! Yet it was too plain that she must and could do nothing. Poor Dan! — and she rose quickly to her feet, frightened at the first sober thought of him. Nothing should make her hurt his feelings again; there was a great gulf between her and the realization of such silly dreams of splendor. Dan was part of herself, and closer than she knew to all her pleasure. An odd, choking tenderness possessed her at the remembrance of his words the last time they had been together. No matter if there were somebody by to hear, the very next time she saw Dan she would tell him how it happened that she had been out in the boat with Mr. Dale Sunday morning. Dan would be sure to come round; he never had been so bad-tempered before, and his fits of anger, ever since she could remember, had been quick to come and quick to go. Dan's honest cheerfulness, his generosity, his merry laughter, were much more familiar than this late uncharacteristic behavior. The situation already seemed less tragical, and by the time her father came to look for her Doris was quite herself again.

Mr. Owen had evidently made a good bargain without any painful preliminaries or opposition, for he was in excellent spirits, and exchanged time-honored jokes with his patron on the propriety of hauling the hay in wet weather, to make it weigh more. The guardian of the place looked at Doris with undisguised admiration, and at parting presented her with a noble bunch of hot-house grapes.

"He makes a sight of money there," said the farmer, as they drove away toward Westmarket. "He's a single man, too," and crafty Israel stole a sly look at his daughter to see if she were displeased, whereupon she laughed aloud, in spite of herself, her hopes and fears, and even her grave responsibilities. All the way to Westmarket they talked with great freedom and satisfaction, and each apparently forgot the constraint that had bound them earlier in the day. They visited a cousin in the town, and enjoyed better than usual the brief association with a more bustling life than was known within the farm limits. Doris's father inclined toward lavish generosity when they were in the shops together, and seemed as pleased as a boy with the holiday. There was a new schooner lying at one of the wharves near the street, and he stopped the horse to take a good look at the pretty craft, with her clean white sails and unused rigging. There were men busy aloft, and hurrying to and fro on the deck. "Seems to me they're in a great drive," said the farmer. "She won't look so smart when they git her back here, if ever. Doris, another year I should n't wonder if you and me and mother went to New York, or somewheres off. She's always desirin' to travel, mother is, and I don't know but 't would keep the barnacles off of us. Young Dale was saying the other day that whenever I•'d come he'd show me all round everywhere, and make me enjoy myself the best he could. What do you say now?" and without waiting for an answer to his enthusiastic proposal, the good man started his horse quickly up the street, as if that were the first stage of such a distinguished journey.

XX.

Supper was an unusually grave occasion that evening, and somehow everybody was made to feel responsible for the general infelicity. Mr. Owen alone made gallant attempts to be cheerful and talkative, but his wife did not come to the table at all, being pretentiously busy in the outer kitchen, and still in that frame of mind which did not invite friendly intercourse. The artist had been far afield all the afternoon, but, contrary to his usual habit, he put away his sketches without displaying them, and came down from the studio after dark, looking quite frost-bitten. The weather had grown very bleak and cold toward night, and the farmer several times bewailed the effect of a possible black frost upon his ungathered fruit. There was, altogether, a disheartening suggestion of approaching winter, and even the door of the outer kitchen, which Mrs. Owen kept throwing open in a willful, aggressive way, admitted a provoking draught of chilly air.

If Doris were chief offender of the family peace, her companions could not find it hard to be forgiving: she never had been more appealing in her gentleness and power of attraction. The bit of morning-glory vine still clung to her belt; the leaves were hardly wilted, and the lamp-light brought out a faint fleck of color on one of the crumpled blossoms. She felt a strange sense of security, as if she had come to a quiet place in the current which had so lately swept her along and beaten her to and fro. This evening was like a peaceful reach of still water; indeed, her thoughts kept wandering back to the quiet August night when she had waited for the haymakers at the landing-place, before the first sign had been given of any misunderstanding between Dan and herself. The soft air, the faint color of the western sky, the sweet notes of the thrushes, — she remembered everything with a glow of pleasure, and smiled more than once unconsciously. The slight change and restfulness of the holiday had done her good, and Dick thought she had not looked so serene and untroubled for many an evening before. Her father gave a pleased glance at Doris from time to time, after he had wisely relapsed into silence. He ate his supper with an excellent appetite; but Dale felt himself upon the brink of a crisis, and pushed back his chair presently without a word, and went into the clock-room. Temperance made great eyes at the half-opened door, and shook her head as if in mournful foreboding; while Israel Owen gave a reproachful look in his wife's direction, as if to say accusingly that she had been destroying the household peace and harmony in his absence. In this disagreeable moment of suspense and uncertainty Temperance took a candle from the high mantel-piece, and disappeared down the cellar stairs; raising a hymn as she went, as if to protect her from evil spirits on her way. The farmer and Doris looked at each other with amused sympathy; there was something so absurdly unnecessary and incongruous in the outburst of psalmody. Temperance must have had the boldness of a pirate, but it was impossible for two of her audience not to accept the diversion with gratitude.

The light from the kitchen shone bright into the clock-room, where there was only a newly kindled fire on the hearth of the Franklin stove, and Dick summoned his host to join him in a comforting evening smoke. It was a serious loss that they could no longer keep each other company on the side-door step, for their conversation had become more conventional since they had been shut within four walls. The farmer was always sympathetic in his moods, and tilted himself backward in his chair now, while they both looked toward the kitchen; it may have been that one was as glad as the other when Doris flitted before the doorway. "Where's Jim Fales?" they heard her ask; and a surly voice from the outer kitchen made a mysterious reply. If the listeners had only known it, Dan Lester's most ardent champion at present was the mistress of the Marsh Island. She was indignant with everybody, but most of all with Doris, and she said to herself, with ever-increasing decision, that the poor fellow should have his rights. There were no half-way measures with Martha Owen.

"You should come on and make us a visit in the winter," Israel Owen was saying to his guest. "I tell you we keep amazin' warm and comfortable here, to what some folks can."

"Warm!" exclaimed Mrs. Owen, who

looked in disapprovingly at that moment. "I should think you had been burning up the chopping-block now. I'm all of a roast." Dick did not know why, but he had never had such a consciousness of being a foreigner as that night; he was like a cinder in the family eye, and it winked and winked, in the hope of dismissing him. He even felt like an interloper suddenly discovered at the meeting of a secret society. They were all linked together by their prejudices and interests, after all, these friendly Owens, and would no more lend themselves for his idle observation and picture-making, being intent upon their own more important concerns. He, Dick Dale, was out of place; but where was his place? What had been the use of him, and what would be his fate? A man who has been led and encouraged by fortune to complacently avail himself of all sorts of rights and favors is suddenly brought face to face with his duties: what then? Dick, who had always thought a great deal of what he meant to do, was forced to contemplate with great dismay the things he had not done. Fortune had unkindly deserted him, and left him in deep water, after a most inadequate swimming lesson. He was sensitive to such convicting moods and misgivings, and suffered deeply when the demands of life and reproaches of conscience showed him his shortcomings. He had not aimed at reaching one goal, — there had seemed rather to be a succession of goals; and happily at this point there dawned upon his mind a suspicion that all these were simply stations on his great highway, and perhaps he was going in the right direction, after all. That very day a letter had come from Bradish, announcing that he and a few comrades would join Dick at the Marsh Island for a week. There was yet time for such a pilgrimage. They could catch the last tints of the autumn foliage, and no doubt on such marshes there was the best of gunning. In the time of coots, therefore, and of ducks and snipe, they might be expected. Of course the cheerful farmer would stow them away somewhere, and they would not steal Dale's material; they would only look him over, and have a jolly week together. Dick had already answered such inflammatory proposals; he had sent Jim Fales away, on his own responsibility, to the nearest post-office with the letter. To-morrow he would dismantle the spinning-room studio, and the next day he would go back to town; and so the good time would be over with. No doubt the fellows would make it an excuse for a supper when he put in an appearance, and a sickening dislike to the aimless, silly routine of existence possessed this young man whom almost everybody envied and admired. Then Dick lifted his head, and, with his eyes a little dazzled by looking at the glowing coals of the fire, took a good view of the old-fashioned room. The farmer was dozing in the high-backed rocking-chair at his side. Temperance and Doris had joined them, and were talking together in low tones by the lamp. Oh, that beautiful Doris! The truth was that he felt powerless to keep the reins of his self-control; it was all nonsense to pretend to himself that he must go away from her to make sure. He belonged here as much as anywhere, and he could not make a fool of himself any longer. The shape of her head was something exquisite; the sound of her voice thrilled him through and through, and he grew unbearably impatient. No more meditation and philosophy and vague plans for him, with such a woman as this, such a love as theirs might be! No; he would stay until

Doris said she would give herself to him, and then they would go out into the wide world together. Here she would be undeveloped on every side save that of the affections, but he could give her the sort of life for which nature had made her fit. One thing had been proved to him by his short absence: that he longed to see her again, and longed to put her in her rightful place, among the books and pictures and silks, among the thoughtful, beauty-loving, and progressive people with whom his own life had been associated. He did not know that Doris herself had been thinking of many things that very day, as she sat on the step of the great house, with the sound of the sea in her ears. He would not have been willing to believe that her serenity to-night came from her decision, instinctive as it was, and almost unrecognized, that she did not belong to the existence or the surroundings so familiar to him, — that there was an unlikeness which never could be bridged over between her and himself.

But some unsilenced monitor kept soberly telling Dick Dale to wait, something kept holding him back; a lack of trust in his own sincerity stung this flower of passion at

17

its heart, and it was already beginning to
fade. He had spent a miserable day, poor
Dick, as must any man who fears that his
love may prove his fall. As for the man
who through his love had hoped to rise, he
also had been wretched. Doris, the woman
around whom so much revolved, on whom so
much depended, seemed calm enough; but
who knows what knowledge of being a pivot,
what fixity and steadfastness, were almost
dulling her sense of responsibility! She felt
her heart beat heavily at every sound from
without the house. It was impossible that
Dan should not come that night; she had
such a sense of his presence that at one moment she was impelled to go out under the
willow boughs, and find him there waiting
in the darkness, wishing only for her, and
dreading to come in to meet her where the
others would watch them curiously. But
how late it was growing! What could be
keeping him! At last, in her excitement
and suspense, she rose, as if the room were
too hot, and went to the side-doorway. Indeed, there was a step close by, and Doris
started back. "Oh, Jim Fales, is that you?"
she said sharply, a moment afterward, and
went on to the kitchen, where her mother sat

in surly silence, mending the family stockings, which service she never allowed any one else to perform, and always did herself as if it were a penance.

Jim Fales came blundering in with an air of great consequence, and threw his hat on the floor, beside the chair which he drew before the kitchen stove. "Got some news now, I guess," he announced, looking at Martha Owen, who did not vouchsafe the slightest notice of him. "I heard as I come along that Dan Lester's been and shipped for the Banks. They was short o' hands for that new schooner that's just rigged and ready, and he up and said he wanted to go a v'y'ge. If I wa'n't promised here I do' know but I'd gone along too," and Jim looked round, slightly dismayed by the silence of his audience. Temperance was standing in the doorway behind him, casting glances at Doris, who looked shocked and white. "I see Dan myself, as I come along," said Jim, as if he had kept the best of his news to the last. Mrs. Owen had condescended to lay her stocking down. "He had been home to say good-by to the old lady, I expect. Don't know how he settled with her; she always has been so against his follerin' the sea, they said. P'r'aps he was here earlier?" asked the lad suddenly, with a crestfallen countenance. It would be a dreadful blow if he were telling an old story, after all.

"No," said Temperance briskly; and everybody was grateful to her for not being stricken with speechlessness, — "no, we 've seen nothing of him hereabouts. When d' you hear they was going to sail?"

"Quick 's they can git away; some said 't was to-morrow mornin' at daybreak," — and Doris turned her face toward the window. "Oh, Dan, Dan!" she thought, as if calling his name in such an agony of pity and remorse would be enough to bring him back again.

"The hoss was peltin' right along, I tell you," pursued Jim Fales. "'Where ye goin'?' says I, and he kind of hauled up and went slow for a minute. 'That you?' says he, and I says Yes; and he waited, kind of, and then says he, 'How 's all the folks?' and I told him we was smart, and asked him when he calc'lated Bangs's schooner was goin' to sail; and he says to-morrow, early. They wanted to get her off by daybreak, if 't was so they could. He was goin' right over then; he 'd promised to do a little job for the cap'n before they went to sea. 'T was only a minute he stopped, and then drove right along. Gorry! I wished I'd asked him who he was goin' to let keep his hoss. I'd rather have that colt than any *I* see go by. 'T ain't none o' your Canady lunkheads, that colt ain't!"

But nobody responded to Jim's enthusiasm. Dick Dale followed the farmer to the kitchen, after a minute's reflection and an unworthy feeling of elation and of triumph over his rival. " Dear, dear!" said Mr. Owen ruefully as if to Dick alone. " Hot haste makes a long road back. Well, 't is a great pity. I would n't have believed Dan could be such a fool. He's master of a good trade to help him out, and he's got good prospects ashore, but he's of a mind to throw 'em to the four winds, — that's plain."

Martha Owen looked at nobody, and drudged away at her stocking. Dale knew that he was unwelcome. He meekly went back to the clock-room, and listened with a sense of personal responsibility to the murmur of voices which began directly after Jim Fales's heavy boots had been dropped behind the stove, and he had gone softly up the back stairs to bed. Jim must be up early in the morning, in these cider-making days. There was something absurd in the lack of disguise as to the state of affairs. In a city household there would have been a thin icing of general conversation over the dangerous depths of such a misfortune, but here the stranger was not considered, and indeed was made to feel his evident agency in bringing about the disaster. "I don't care who hears me," said his hostess once, in a raised voice, which came as straight to Dick's ears as if there had been no others on the way: "Dan ought n't to have been drove away from his rights. He's just come into a handsome property in the West, and nobody knows whether there'll be a straw of it left when he gets back, if ever he does;" and at this point somebody — Dick thought it might be Doris herself — came nearer, and shut the kitchen door.

Dick was thoroughly uncomfortable. He was ashamed to quietly disappear, and hide himself in his bed at that early hour. He took one of his own books from the table, and tried to read; but the situation was too startling a combination of tragedy and comedy. It was something, however, to preserve the appearance of a devotion to literature when Temperance reappeared. She looked at him as if he were a blameless but mistaken baby, who had played with matches and beggared its family. When Mr. Richard Dale tried to behave as if nothing had happened, and, looking at his own sketch of the young soldier which hung on the wall before him, ventured at last to say that the younger Israel must have been a fine fellow and a terrible loss, Temperance clicked her knitting-needles vindictively, and made no reply.

"It is a glorious thing to die for one's country," Dale added pensively; and this brought his companion to an expression of her opinion. "That's what everybody s'posed they must remark," she snapped; "but I called it a darned shame, and I always shall:" whereupon Dick took up his book again to conceal his quite unexpected revulsion of feeling. He wished, and yet he feared, to see Doris again that night; but she did not appear, and after lingering a while this unhappy stranger and foreigner took a candle and departed. The old clock ticked in a more leisurely fashion than ever that night, as if to keep a check upon the excited household. It had measured off sadder hours than these many times over. Life should not be spoiled by haste or waste; tomorrow would be a new day. Some younger timekeepers might be saying, Hurry, hurry! but this was one that said, Wait, wait!

XXI.

Doris never had known so long a night. Her poor eyes were worn out with tears, for she accused herself a hundred times of being wholly to blame. She had not meant to be faithless or provoking, and yet she had brought down such calamity upon everybody. She tried to think over Dan's grievances as he had evidently seen them, but she failed to convict herself of any real fault. She liked Mr. Dale ; she enjoyed the pleasantness and novelty of the new interests his coming had brought. She had dreamed a little, as girls will, of her future if she should love him. There had been times when she did not shrink from the new atmosphere that had surrounded the young artist and herself, and the remembrance of one moment under the beech-tree would always keep a tender place for him in her heart. But she knew now once for all that she never could belong to anybody but Dan, and Dan was angry with her ; he was putting his dear life in peril all for a foolish mistake. The girl was long at her prayers in the cold little chamber. She shivered and cried. She feared, as she never had feared anything before, that this handsome, reckless fellow would be drowned, if he went to sea. She remembered his sad old mother, and grew every hour more alarmed and hopeless. At last she thought of a plan, — or to her it was like the bidding of an angel: she would go herself to Westmarket in the morning, and find Dan Lester, and beg him to stay at home.

The moonlight was clear and bright, and many times Doris looked out of her narrow window to see if there were any signs of dawn. She must get to the schooner by daylight, if she were to be in time. They would be likely to sail at high water from that wharf, for the harbor was shallow near by. She counted the hours, and laid her plan with the intensity of one out of her reason; though once, when from very weariness the exigency of it faded away, it seemed to poor Doris as if the punishment for her fault and foolishness were out of all proportion to its deserts. And if Dan were so unreasonable and jealous the worst was his own. The next minute a sense of his great love, a love that had always been growing, and of his bitter disappointment made her cry with pity for him and for herself. How could they live through so many wretched, silent weeks apart! Perhaps these fishermen, like many others, would never be heard from after they left port; for many a schooner, Doris knew, had been ploughed under by the great prow of a steamship, its little light gone out through carelessness, and the sleeping men drowned in the sea and lost, as if it were a bad dream of danger mingled with their dreams of home.

It was still night when Doris left her comfortless bed, and stepping carefully about the room, so that she would wake nobody, dressed herself in her warmest clothes. Her heart was breaking with fear and shame together. She had determined at last not to wake her father or Jim, to beg them to go with her to Westmarket; neither would she wait even to drive along the highway, as if this were any other errand. The remembrance of the shorter distance across the marshes to the town filled her mind wholly. It was already four o'clock; she had heard the great timekeeper count it out slowly, and there was not a minute to lose. Enough time had been wasted already in fruitless self-reproaches and bewailings, and the relief of action under so great a sense of disaster was a blessing in itself. A little later the girl was fairly out-of-doors, — outside the silent house, outside all protection and precedent also, as if she had been launched off the face of this familiar earth, and must find her way unwelcomed and unheralded through space.

The frost had fallen, and glistened white along the trodden pathway that led up through the dooryard. The window of the spinning-room caught the moonlight, and flashed in her face as she passed by; and Doris turned once and looked at the old house, as if she were asking forgiveness, and wondering if life would ever be the same to her after this dreadful night. She thought of her soldier brother, and wondered, too, if he had not sometimes been brave alone at night, like this, and so would keep her company in love and pity. Oh, there were so many reasons why she must get to Dan in time! Everybody would guess his reason for going; everybody would talk of it, and laugh, and watch her until he came back, and blame her forever, for his poor mother's sake, if he were lost. In time of war and peril women had done such things as this, but Doris could not think of herself as heroic. She only repented the sins for which she must be blamed if she did not get to Westmarket before the schooner sailed. Out of her quiet life and simple thoughts, troubled with pain and sorrow of the keenest sort, she hurried away into the night. After one great shiver she did not feel cold again, but hurried, hurried, over the crisp gray grass, down across the long, clean-swept field, where the moon, sinking low in the sky, hindered her with a trailing shadow that seemed to delay her more and more.

There was a high tide of treacherous-looking water, and when she came to the brink of it she stopped an instant, as if hesitating. The creek was wide here, and it never had looked half so far across; but Doris went carefully along the shore until she came to an old boat, which had been on many an errand, but never in all its life had carried a young girl alone on a night like this. Before long she was afloat. The boat leaked and went heavily; the oars that she had pulled from their familiar hiding-place were short and heavy, and splintering at their handles. But Doris rowed as if this were a race, and looked often over her shoulder, until at last she heard the dry sedges of the farther shore rustle and bend, and she could step on dry land and be on her way again.

The dawn was glimmering in the east; the moon was almost down; the whole country lay dead and still, as if it would not live again with the morning. Beyond the marshes which Doris must cross there were great drifts of bleached white sand, as if the ghosts of the night had transformed the world to their color, and it had hardly regained its own again. It was a dead fragment of the world, at any rate, — a field where little grew that needed more than rain and air. Doris kept her eyes fixed on the sand dunes, and they appeared to recede as she advanced, mocking her like a mirage, and at last coming close when she thought they were still far away. At length her feet stumbled in the white, shifting, slipping heaps, and she toiled and crept upon them, so slowly, so disappointingly; for they seemed to be planted there as a barrier, raised by enchantment. Alas! this night was all enchantment. Where was the sunshiny yesterday, when she had been secure and peaceful, and almost happy, when one compared those hours with these?

The sky was clear in the east, and fast growing brighter; but each way Doris looked, there was only this desert waste of sand, white as bone, deep and bewildering, and the coarse grass and hungry heather clung to the higher heaps of it here and there. It was like a picture of the misery and emptiness of the girl's future, if her lover went away to sea. For the first time she grew afraid, and her strength left her suddenly, while she looked ahead to where, across more sand and more water and a long slope of upland pastures, the spires of Westmarket were already catching the color of the sunrise. Beside her were some old apple-trees that the shifting dunes had waged war against and defeated. They were discouraged and forlorn in their desolation, like the fig-tree that was cursed. Doris looked pityingly at their dead leaves and mossy tangle of branches; and at that moment a withered, pathetic mockery of fruit fell on the sand at her feet. It was like a conscious gift from these outlawed growths; it somehow gave her a bit of sympathy. Did they indeed know the bitterness of loneliness and the withdrawal of everything that makes life comfortable and dear? They had been walled in and condemned to death, the poor trees, though away in the world people were making merry fearlessly under the same great empty sky.

As the light grew clearer little tracks of birds and small wild creatures could be seen on the drifted sand. Once Doris surprised a fox that was stealing along through the hollows of the dunes. He was hardly startled; he only changed his course a little, and went gliding down toward the marshes, with his brush trailing after him. Doris felt as if she were a wild creature, too. She tried to remind herself of other days than this, to keep her wits together. She wondered once, if she should faint and fall here, how long it would be before any one would come and find her, or if they had missed her yet; her mother and Temperance would be sure to wake her early on this unhappy morning. She thought of herself as if she were still at home in her warm bed under the blue and white counterpane. She dreaded the sound of heavy footsteps in the entry outside. They might leave her to herself that one day, until Mr. Dale and Jim, and even her father, were out of-the house. And all the while she was flitting on, on, over the white desert, with a chill autumn sky above her, with a fox and the wondering birds of the air for company.

When she gained the shore of the last inlet, all seemed lost! She had not thought how she could cross there; and she stopped still and looked about her, hoping in vain to see a boat. It was too late to retrace her steps, and go round by the neck of land that joined the sand wastes to some marshes and the mainland; and she sat down, and covered her face with her hands. The tears would come, because she was so tired and so desperate; she had not thought of crying before, but now it was a great comfort. "O God, help me!" said poor Doris, over and over again, and for one moment Dick Dale's eyes looked into hers again, with that same dazzle. If he were only here, he would help her, — anything would be better than this. He was so gentle! But her thoughts went roving away again to her own dear Dan. How many things she had learned of Mr. Dale which she could do for him by and by!

Dan would like to have the house pleasant. Dan had a pretty taste, and his mother had always said that his fingers were as quick as a woman's. She should always be sorry that he had not seen Mr. Dale's pictures; he would have liked them better than anybody. Oh, if she were only at home! She never could go all the way back, and they would hunt for her soon, and grow frightened when she could not be found. How could she face them all when she got home? By that time Dan would be out of the harbor. How could he be so angry! — and Doris wished she could die there, and never open her eyes again upon this miserable world.

As the sun rose, a weather-beaten boat, with two boys for crew, came down the river. They were enjoying a stolen pleasure, and it was not surprising to them that in a time of such excitement and tremendous consequence a strange young woman, with a white, scared face, should call to them from the farther shore and ask to be set across. Their cheerful voices and red cheeks and their air of mystery and adventure did Doris good, and she put them on the track of the fox with their clumsy gun, and wished them a fine day's sport. They looked at her furtively as they tugged the old boat through the water; they watched her quickly climb the low hill that rose between them and the town.

It was a bright, sunshiny morning at last, — just the day to begin a voyage. The blue sea sparkled, and dazzled the eyes that looked eastward from the high ground, from whence one could overlook the village roofs and chimneys, with the line of masts between them and the narrow harbor beyond. At one place and another there were white sails hoisted, and a fleet of fishing-smacks were making ready to go out with the tide. As the wives and mothers of the fishermen were astir early in the little town, some of them tearful enough already, they might have seen a slender figure making its way to the shore. They did not know what a fear-stricken, heavy heart was passing by their windows, or how much need of comfort the young stranger had that morning. Would she be too late, after all? Was Dan beyond her reach even now? The schooners would drift quickly away from their moorings, the sails unfurl themselves to the fresh westerly breeze. Unless she could hurry along the harbor side and put off in a dory, there was no chance left, and a vision of the mocking faces of the sailors, and even of Dan's displeasure, made Doris hesitate for one dismayed instant; then she hurried on again. The street looked endlessly long; she felt as if she were in a nightmare, and a dreadful dullness made her go more and more slowly. At last she came near the wharf; round the next corner she could see —

"Doris! Here, *Doris!*" and for a minute the girl looked bewildered, and the light faded in her eyes. Somebody was coming across the street, also to make his way down the lane that led to the water-side. Could it be Dan himself, in his every-day clothes? There never was a stranger sight; and yet this was truly Dan, not gone to sea at all. Were they there, where nobody was watching them, instead of at the harbor, where people could flout at such a scene?

"Oh, Dan," said the girl faintly, "please take me home as quick as you can. I thought you — Jim Fales said you were going to the George's Banks. I did n't mean to make you feel bad" —

"Take right hold of my arm," said Dan. "Come, we 'd better go home, Doris," as if she had been a child. "I love the ground you step on, darlin'. How did you get over here this time o' day? I " — But Dan faltered, and could say no more. He thought it would never do for him to cry there in the street, even if Doris were draggled and wet, and looked so pinched and cold; even, as he knew a little later, if she had come across the marshes, Heaven only knew how, for his unworthy sake.

XXII.

When the lovers drove into the farm-house yard, they were greeted with mingled expressions of relief and astonishment. Dan was instantly received as a member of the family, for it was unmistakable that the young folks had in some way or other "made it up between them." "I must say you have led us a pretty dance," Mrs. Owen said, with a cheerful, bantering air, to her daughter. "We never missed you till just now. I thought likely you was sleeping late, after driving so far yesterday. Now, Dan, I hope Doris and your mother together have persuaded you out o' such school-boy nonsense as goin' fishin'?" There could be detected a slight impatience with the girl, who was believed to have stolen away so early in the morning to join forces with her lover's mother. Mrs. Owen herself would never have stooped to such a thing, but this was no time to make a bad impression upon so prosperous and evidently victorious a son-in-law.

She had been too fearful of losing him the night before.

Doris stole upstairs, grateful and bewildered, but longing only to be quiet for a while. She felt as if she had left the familiar room years ago instead of a few hours, all her life was so changed. The sweet warmth of the sun was pouring in at the window; some late flies buzzed at the panes, as if they wished to escape and share the freedom of the bright October day. Doris heard her lover's voice now and then. It seemed like a Sunday morning out-of-doors. Her thoughts went backward with wonder and delight, finding in every memory some proof and assurance that she and Dan were born to love each other. Their happiness had suddenly burst into bloom; but for all that, the flower's roots had been growing unseen in the darkness, and even the misunderstanding, of the past.

Later, with an air of unusual hilarity, Temperance went out to meet Jim Fales, as he came loitering home from the pasture and a prolonged experience of salting sheep. "Jim Fales," she inquired, with mysterious deference, " I s'pose you don't know of a wanderin' minister of the Orthodox persuasion anywhere about?"

"Lor', yes," said Jim promptly, equal to a joke, but puzzling his brains for the meaning of this. "Got occasion for one right away, Temperance? Who've you picked out since I've been gone?" while at that moment his eyes fell upon Israel Owen and Dan Lester, who were leaning over the garden fence together in friendly intercourse.

Temperance gave an emphatic nod, as her colleague opened his eyes very wide and whistled a wild note; then she turned back toward the house, wearing her most circumspect expression. Her great checked apron fluttered and bulged in the breeze; she seemed to be looking down intently at some white geese feathers that had caught in the dry grass stalks, and were floating lightly like tiny flags of truce. One of the cats came running to meet her. Mrs. Owen was standing in the kitchen doorway, very amiable and friendly, it was plain to see, and offering no apparent objections to a good talk. Young Fales directed his steps toward the barn door, where he had observed the wheels of Lester's buggy, and there he passed a season of wonder and enjoyment. The vehicle bore traces of having been driven at uncommon speed, and the horse, a swift young creature, was drooping his head, and still breathing faster than usual. "Here's some of that blamed red mud that comes from most over to Westmarket," meditated the curious lad. " He's given up goin' fishin', that's plain enough;" and Jim wandered into the kitchen, brimful of sincere interest and good-will, only to be promptly dismissed by Martha Owen, and blamed for hanging round at that time in the morning, when there was everything to be done. "Ain't he goin' to sea?" asked the lad, with uncalled-for sympathy in his tone, and the two women smiled at each other.

"I guess he was only talkin' about it," volunteered Temperance, evidently much amused; but Mrs. Owen gravely explained that Dan's mother was set against it from the first, and Dan himself gave up the notion when he came to find out what kind of a crew they'd shipped.

The triumphant lover stayed to dinner, and that was a day of high festival at the farm, although there were few outward signs of the satisfaction and rejoicing. After a short absence Dan returned with his mother, both dressed in their best, and there was much hand-shaking among the men and a few kisses and tears to show the women's approval. Nobody spoke directly of the great event, — perhaps the Marsh Island's vocabulary did not contain any form of speech for such deep thoughts; but the little group talked together about Dan's Western prospects, as if they were one family already in very truth. Mr. Dale was not slow to offer his congratulations. He tried to forget that there had been the slightest cloud of discomfort over the sky; he imagined that he found it very charming at the studio, and that it seemed more like the first part of his residence on the island than the last. Dick was very sympathetic: he could not help being glad that everybody else was so happy, and there was a certain sort of relief in finding that there was no serious decision to be made after all, and that he had been mistaken in his consciousness of an uncommon responsibility and need of action. He could not bear the thought of Doris's narrow future; perhaps, if the truth were told, he was more concerned for her sake than for his own. And yet —

At supper-time Dick expressed much sorrow to his entertainers because he could not linger a week later. He should like to carry away a sketch or two of the cider-making, having just passed the press at their neighbor Bennet's, and joined the friendly company that surrounded it. He was deeply touched when Mr. Owen turned to him, with an affectionate look, and said, "I must say I hate to part with you, my lad."

"I expect he'll be a great man one of these days," added Mrs. Owen politely. "You must always make it your home here, if you come this way, Mr. Dale. You must n't get to feelin' above us." After this it seemed to Dick as if the sooner he were gone the better.

That afternoon, as he was putting his sketches together in the spinning-room, he thought a good deal about Doris. He had not seen her since the day before, but he had won a confession of her morning journey from the wistful old father, who alternated complete delight with compassion for even the happy young people themselves. "They don't know life as I know it. But I 've calc'lated for a considerable spell on havin' Dan take holt of the farm. He could n't help weepin', Dan could n't, — an' I don' know 's I blame him, — when he was tellin' how Doris come after him. He made me promise that I nor nobody else should n't ever hint a word about it to her."

Dick nodded. There was no use in saying that he believed the beautiful girl capable of any heroism and masterly scope of achievement, as he knew her equality to all refinements and tenderness. He was bitterly ashamed of his deliberations. He wished more than ever that a strong tide might have assailed him and swept him off the shore where mistaken reason or any aspect of worldliness had given insecure foothold. Doris had seemed younger than her years, and had painted herself upon his consciousness in pale colors, and faint, though always perfectly defined, outlines. But his old knowledge of her seemed now as the enthusiasm and eagerness of a first sketch does to the dignity and fine assertion of a finished picture. One could say easily that Doris and Dan Lester were destined for each other, and console one's self by thinking there was never any chance to win. Alas for those who let the golden moment pass, — who let the gate of opportunity be shut in their faces, while they wait before it trying to muster favoring conditions, or argument and authority, like an army with banners to escort them through.

Farmer Owen thought that Dick looked a good deal older than when he came, as he shook hands with the young man and said good-by. "There, it always seemed more like having a girl about than a man," said the mistress of the Marsh Island, as she watched the wagon, already almost out of sight far down the road. "I expect we shall miss him considerable, he was so pleasant. I believe he took to Doris more 'n he 'd let on. I should n't wonder if he sent her somethin' real handsome for a weddin' present."

"He won't never set the river afire," said Temperance, whose countenance wore a most regretful and sentimental expression. "He wants to have all the town ladders out to git him over a grain o' sand."

"I tell you he's got good grit, now!" exclaimed Mr. Owen fiercely; "there's more to him than you think for. He ain't got a brow an' eye so like pore Israel's all for nothin'. He promised he'd write an' tell me when he'd been an' voted to this next election, too," added the farmer, who was a conscientious politician. "No wonder the country's been goin' to the dogs, when such folks don't think it's wuth their while to take holt." But as the little company separated each could have told the other that Dick's going away reminded them of a far sadder day, not many years before.

XXIII.

"Good-morning, my melancholy Jaques!" said Mr. Bradish, a day or two afterward, looking up from his easel at a friend who had strayed into the studio as if he had left it only an hour or two before. "Are you sure there was no malaria in your paradise?"

Bradish was a sedate-looking young gentleman, with a roundish head, and short black hair, and pathetic brown eyes. He almost never laughed, he rarely even smiled, but he was always called the prince of good fellows by his comrades. There is a well-known chemical process, called the action of presence, where a certain substance produces a radical change in others, but remains unaffected itself. Bradish could make everybody else laugh and take a cheerful view of life. You smiled at the mere sight of him, as if he were some great comedian. At that moment his financial affairs had reached an unprecedented crisis, and he rejoiced to see his best ally at hand, though he painted busily, and apparently paid Dick no further attention for some minutes.

"You might have given a poor beggar a chance," he asserted presently. "I have had frightful luck all summer."

"That sketch does n't look like it," said Dick, coming nearer, and stepping to and fro to get a better light. "That's better than ever, Bradish, — a first-rate blow-away sky. What's going on? I feel like a hermit dropped down into the middle of the theatre. I came near waiting half the afternoon out here on the sidewalk, to let the crowd get by."

"Welcome home, my love," said Bradish, in a delightful tone of voice. "You must give away those clothes, you know."

"Another aunt of mine frowned upon them," responded Dale meditatively, as he went sauntering about the room. "But wait until I show you my sketches. Ah, here's the box from the farm, now! When did it get here? You would have just lost your head completely. It really was a lovely old place. I used to wish for you with all my heart."

"I thought so."

"Oh, never mind nonsense," and Dick's voice had a strange eagerness. Jim Fales had reckoned on the perils of travel when he drove the nails, and the comrades worked together diligently to loosen them. Dick had not anticipated the little shock, almost like pain, that the sight of his pictures would give him. Life at the farm seemed already very far away. Here was the first sketch of the birch-tree, the willows, and the wide outlook across the green marshes. It was odd that this should have come uppermost, and he held it off and looked at it without a word, while Bradish admired the pretty landscape with eager friendliness.

"This was only the first," said Dale. "I feel like Rip Van Winkle. Look them over, if you like, and say the worst you can. I've had a good solid bit of life, at any rate. It was a good thing to get a look at such a permanent institution as that farm and its inhabitants. I felt all the time like an accident, an ephemeral sort of existence; but I believe we are all a sort of two-stalked vegetable, with a power of locomotion that ought not to be too severely taxed."

Bradish groaned. "I hoped you would forsake your philosophy, when I found you had really taken to painting," he said, and gave his attention to the contents of the flat box. "You rich fellows are always lucky," he added ruefully, a little later, after his enthusiasm had cooled enough to allow his thoughts to express themselves. "The avarice of you in keeping such a mine to yourself was despicable, but there 'll be a convention of us there next summer. Of course you even fell in love with the daughter?"

"No," said Dick slowly, — "no. But I wish I had, Bradish, if you want the simple truth."

"I should be wishing I had n't," answered Bradish, with great gravity. "Cry a little, Dale; it will do you good."

Yet Dick, who was always ready to be amused at his friend's jokes, did not even smile. If there were any difference, existence was a more serious thing now he was back in town than it had been at the Sussex farm. Whether the warmth of his feeling for Doris Owen was equal or not to changing the iron of his character into steel, he was dimly conscious that for each revelation of truth or beauty Heaven demands tribute and better service than before. He had at least gained a new respect for his own life and its possible value.

One day in midwinter Doris went away by herself for a long walk over the crusted snow. She climbed the hill, and looked out across the marshes. They seemed larger than in summer, and there were black cracks in the ice, like scars. She wished that it were spring again, and thought eagerly of all the work she meant to do; being, indeed, happier as a wife than she had ever been as a maiden, and just beginning the very best of her days. The night before, a shower of rain had frozen as it fell, and the world was all sparkling and glistening, as if it were a great arctic holiday. The sky was a clear, dazzling blue, and the air was still and cold. Doris Lester thought of Mr. Dale, and with a quick sympathy imagined how much he would like to see this fantastic, ice-bound country. She could see through and through his feeling for her now, but she knew that he had not gone away and forgotten her; and half wistfully she gave a glance at the smaller island where she had found him asleep on the Sunday morning.

Dan and her father had gone away early in the day to visit a distant piece of woodland, and just as she reached the house they drove into the yard.

"I expected you 'd have to go out to see the trees, Doris," said the elder man, smiling. "Don't they look handsome? I wished you was with us up in the country where there's more growth; but I declare, it's as pretty a place here as 't is anywhere."

"I tell you we 're just going to make the old farm hum next summer," said Lester, as he stepped out of the high-backed sleigh; but his companion did not follow him at once. "I 've got a New York paper in my pocket," Israel Owen told the little audience. "Young Mr. Dale sent it to me, and he marked a place that tells about his pictures being exhibited with the rest of the folks', and that they all come round his like a swarm of bees. There's a long piece about 'em."

Mrs. Owen was listening eagerly. "Now, Doris!" she said. "Don't you wish you was there, a-queenin' it?" But Doris and Dan gave each other a happy look that was answer enough. They could not imagine anything better than life was that very day on their own Marsh Island.

Works of Fiction

PUBLISHED BY

HOUGHTON, MIFFLIN AND COMPANY,

4 Park St., Boston; 11 E. 17th St., New York.

Thomas Bailey Aldrich.

Story of a Bad Boy. Illustrated. 12mo	$1.50
Marjorie Daw and Other People. 12mo	1.50
The Same. Riverside Aldine Series. 16mo	1.00
Prudence Palfrey. 12mo	1.50
The Queen of Sheba. 12mo	1.50
The Stillwater Tragedy. 12mo	1.50

Hans Christian Andersen.

Complete Works. In ten uniform volumes, crown 8vo.

The Improvisatore; or, Life in Italy	1.50
The Two Baronesses	1.50
O. T.; or, Life in Denmark	1.50
Only a Fiddler	1.50
In Spain and Portugal	1.50
A Poet's Bazaar	1.50
Pictures of Travel	1.50
The Story of my Life. With portrait	1.50
Wonder Stories told for Children. Illustrated	1.50
Stories and Tales. Illustrated	1.50
The set	15.00
A new and cheap Edition, in attractive binding. Sold only in sets	10.00

William Henry Bishop.

Detmold: A Romance. "Little Classic" style. 18mo	1.25
The House of a Merchant Prince. 12mo	1.50
Choy Susan, and other Stories. 16mo	1.25

Works of Fiction Published by

Björnstjerne Björnson.
Works. *American Edition*, sanctioned by the author, and translated by Professor R. B. Anderson, of the University of Wisconsin. In seven volumes, 16mo.

Synnöve Solbakken.
Arne.
A Happy Boy.
The Fisher Maiden.
The Bridal March, and Other Stories.
Captain Mansana, and Other Stories.
Magnhild.
    Each volume $1.00
    The set 7.00
    The Same. In three volumes, 12mo 4.50

Alice Cary.
Pictures of Country Life. 12mo 1.50

John Esten Cooke.
My Lady Pokahontas. 16mo 1.25

James Fenimore Cooper.
Complete Works. New *Household Edition*, in attractive binding. With Introductions to many of the volumes by Susan Fenimore Cooper, and Illustrations. In thirty-two volumes, 16mo.

Precaution.	The Prairie.
The Spy.	Wept of Wish-ton-Wish.
The Pioneers.	The Water Witch.
The Pilot.	The Bravo.
Lionel Lincoln.	The Heidenmauer.
Last of the Mohicans.	The Headsman.
Red Rover.	The Monikins.
Homeward Bound.	Miles Wallingford.
Home as Found.	The Red Skins.
The Pathfinder.	The Chainbearer.
Mercedes of Castile.	Satanstoe.
The Deerslayer.	The Crater.
The Two Admirals.	Jack Tier.
Wing and Wing.	The Sea Lions.
Wyandotté.	Oak Openings.
Afloat and Ashore.	The Ways of the Hour.

(*Each volume sold separately.*)

    Each volume 1.00
    The set 32.00
    Half calf 80.00

Houghton, Mifflin and Company.

Fireside Edition. With thirty-two original Illustrations by Darley, Dielman, Fredericks, Sheppard, and Waud. In sixteen volumes, 12mo.
    The set $20.00
    Half calf 43.00
        (*Sold only in sets.*)

Sea Tales. New *Household Edition*, in attractive binding, the volumes containing Introductions by Susan Fenimore Cooper. Illustrated.
  First Series. Including —
  The Pilot.   The Red Rover.
  The Water Witch.   The Two Admirals.
  Wing and Wing.
    Second Series. Including —
  The Sea Lions.   Afloat and Ashore.
  Jack Tier.   Miles Wallingford.
  The Crater.
    Each set, 5 vols. 16mo 5.00
    Half calf 12.50

Leather-Stocking Tales. New *Household Edition*, in attractive binding, the volumes containing Introductions by Susan Fenimore Cooper. Illustrated. In five volumes, 16mo.
  The Deerslayer.   The Pioneers.
  The Pathfinder.   The Prairie.
  Last of the Mohicans.
    The set 5.00
    Half calf 12.50

Cooper Stories; being Narratives of Adventure selected from his Works. With Illustrations by F. O. C. Darley. In three volumes, 16mo, each 1.00

Charles Egbert Craddock.

In the Tennessee Mountains. 16mo 1.25
The Prophet of the Great Smoky Mountains. (*In press.*)
Down the Ravine. A Story for Young People. Illustrated. 16mo 1.00

F. Marion Crawford.

To Leeward. 16mo 1.25
A Roman Singer. 16mo 1.25
An American Politician. 16mo 1.25

Maria S. Cummins.

The Lamplighter. 12mo 1.50
El Fureidîs. 12mo 1.50
Mabel Vaughan. 12mo 1.50

Works of Fiction Published by

Daniel De Foe.
Robinson Crusoe. Illustrations by Thomas Nast and
E. Bayard. 16mo $1.00

P. Deming.
Adirondack Stories. "Little Classic" style. 18mo . .75
Tompkins and other Folks 1.00

Thomas De Quincey.
Romances and Extravaganzas. *Riverside Edition.*
12mo 1.50
Narrative and Miscellaneous Papers. *Riverside Edition.* 12mo 1.50

Charles Dickens.
Complete Works. *Illustrated Library Edition.* With Introductions, biographical and historical, by E. P. Whipple. Containing all the Illustrations that have appeared in the English edition by Cruikshank, Phiz, Seymour, John Leech, Maclise, Marcus Stone, and others, engraved on steel, to which are added the designs of F. O. C. Darley and John Gilbert, in all numbering over 550. Handsomely bound, and complete in twenty-nine volumes, 12mo.

The Pickwick Papers, 2 vols.
Nicholas Nickleby, 2 vols.
Oliver Twist.
Old Curiosity Shop, and Reprinted Pieces, 2 vols.
Barnaby Rudge, and Hard Times, 2 vols.
Martin Chuzzlewit, 2 vols.
Our Mutual Friend, 2 vols.
Uncommercial Traveller.
A Child's History of England, and Other Pieces.
Christmas Books.
Dombey and Son, 2 vols.
Pictures from Italy, and American Notes.
Bleak House, 2 vols.
Little Dorrit, 2 vols.
David Copperfield, 2 vols.
A Tale of Two Cities.
Great Expectations.
Edwin Drood, Master Humphrey's Clock, and Other Pieces.
Sketches by Boz.

Each volume 1.50
The set. With Dickens Dictionary. 30 vols . . 45.00
Half calf 100.00

Globe Edition. Printed in large type (long primer) on good paper, and containing all the Illustrations of Darley and Gilbert (55 in number) on steel, and the Index of Characters. In fifteen volumes, 12mo.
Each volume 1.25
The set 18.75
Half calf, or half morocco 40.00

Christmas Carol. Illustrated. 8vo, full gilt $3.00
    Morocco 7.00
The Same. 32mo 75
Christmas Books. Illustrated. 12mo 2.00
    Morocco 5.00

Edgar Fawcett.
A Hopeless Case. "Little Classic" style. 18mo . 1.25
A Gentleman of Leisure. "Little Classic" style. 18mo 1.00
An Ambitious Woman. 12mo 1.50

Fénelon.
Adventures of Telemachus. 12mo 2.25

Harford Flemming.
A Carpet Knight. 16mo 1.25

Baron de la Motte Fouqué.
Undine, Sintram and his Companions, with St. Pierre's "Paul and Virginia," 32mo 75
Undine and other Tales. Illustrated. "Riverside Classics." 16mo 1.00

Johann Wolfgang von Goethe.
Wilhelm Meister. Translated by Thomas Carlyle. Portrait of Goethe. In two volumes. 12mo . . 3.00
The Tale and Favorite Poems. 32mo 75

Oliver Goldsmith.
Vicar of Wakefield. *Handy-Volume Edition.* 32mo, gilt top 1.25
The Same. "Riverside Classics." Illustrated. 16mo 1.00

Jeanie T. Gould (Mrs. Lincoln).
Marjorie's Quest. Illustrated. 12mo 1.50

Thomas Chandler Haliburton.
The Clockmaker; or, The Sayings and Doings of Samuel Slick of Slickville. "Riverside Classics." Illustrated by Darley. 16mo 1.00

A. S. Hardy.
But Yet a Woman. 16mo 1.25

Miriam Coles Harris.
Rutledge.   A Perfect Adonis.
The Sutherlands.   Missy.
Frank Warrington.   Happy-Go-Lucky.
St. Philips.   Phœbe.
Richard Vandermarck.
Each volume, 12mo 1.25

Works of Fiction Published by

Bret Harte.

The Luck of Roaring Camp, and Other Sketches. 16mo $1.50
The Same. Riverside Aldine Series. 16mo . . . 1.00
Condensed Novels. Illustrated. 16mo 1.50
Mrs. Skaggs's Husbands, and Other Sketches. 16mo. 1.50
Tales of the Argonauts, and Other Stories. 16mo . 1.50
Thankful Blossom. "Little Classic" style. 18mo . 1.25
Two Men of Sandy Bar. A Play. "Little Classic" style. 18mo 1.00
The Story of a Mine. "Little Classic" style. 18mo 1.00
Drift from Two Shores. "Little Classic" style. 18mo 1.25
The Twins of Table Mountain, and Other Sketches. "Little Classic" style. 18mo. 1.25
Works. Rearranged, with an Introduction and a Portrait. In five volumes, crown 8vo.
Poetical Works, and the drama, "Two Men of Sandy Bar," with an Introduction and Portrait.
The Luck of Roaring Camp, and Other Stories.
Tales of the Argonauts and Eastern Sketches.
Gabriel Conroy.
Stories and "Condensed Novels."

    Each volume 2.00
    The set 10.00
    Half calf 20.00

Flip ; and, Found at Blazing Star. "Little Classic" style. 18mo. 1.00
In the Carquinez Woods. "Little Classic" style. 18mo. 1.00
On the Frontier. "Little Classic" style. 18mo . . 1.00
By Shore and Sedge. "Little Classic" style. 18mo 1.00

Nathaniel Hawthorne.

Works. *New Riverside Edition.* With an original etching in each volume, and a new Portrait. With bibliographical notes by George P. Lathrop. Complete in twelve volumes, crown 8vo.
Twice-Told Tales.
Mosses from an Old Manse.
The House of the Seven Gables, and the Snow-Image.
The Wonder-Book, Tanglewood Tales, and Grandfather's Chair.
The Scarlet Letter, and The Blithedale Romance.
The Marble Faun.
Our Old Home, and English Note-Books. 2 vols.
American Note-Books.
French and Italian Note-Books.
The Dolliver Romance, Fanshawe, Septimius Felton, and, in an Appendix, the Ancestral Footstep.

Houghton, Mifflin and Company. 7

Tales, Sketches, and Other Papers. With Biographical Sketch by G. P. Lathrop, and Indexes.
    Each volume $2.00
    The set 24.00
    Half calf 48.00
    Half crushed levant 60.00
"*Little Classic*" *Edition.* Each volume contains a new Vignette Illustration. In twenty-five volumes, 18mo.
    Each volume 1.00
    The set 25.00
    Half calf, or half morocco 62.50
    Tree calf 81.00
A Wonder-Book for Girls and Boys. *Holiday Edition.* With Illustrations by F. S. Church. 4to 2.50
Twice-Told Tales. *School Edition.* 18mo 1.00
The Scarlet Letter. *Holiday Edition.* Illustrated by Mary Hallock Foote. Red-line border. 8vo, full gilt 4.00
    Half calf 6.00
    Morocco, or tree calf 9.00
True Stories from History and Biography. 12mo . 1.50
The Wonder-Book. 12mo 1.50
Tanglewood Tales. 12mo 1.50
Tales of the White Hills, and Legends of New England. 32mo 75
Legends of Province House, and A Virtuoso's Collection. 32mo 75

Oliver Wendell Holmes.
Elsie Venner. A Romance of Destiny. Crown 8vo. 2.00
The Guardian Angel. Crown 8vo 2.00
The Story of Iris. 32mo 75

Blanche Willis Howard.
One Summer. A Novel. "Little Classic" style. 18mo 1.25
Holiday Edition. Illustrated by Hoppin. Square 12mo 2.50

Augustus Hoppin.
Recollections of Auton House. Illustrated. Small 4to 1.25
A Fashionable Sufferer. Illustrated. 12mo . . . 1.50
Two Compton Boys. Illustrated. Square 16mo.

William Dean Howells.
Their Wedding Journey. Illustrated. 12mo . . . 1.50
The Same. Illustrated. Paper covers. 16mo . . .50

Works of Fiction Published by

The Same. "Little Classic" style. 18mo $1.25
A Chance Acquaintance. Illustrated. 12mo . . . 1.50
The Same. Illustrated. Paper covers. 16mo . . .50
The Same. "Little Classic" style. 18mo 1.25
A Foregone Conclusion. 12mo 1.50
The Lady of the Aroostook. 12mo 1.50
The Undiscovered Country. 12mo 1.50
A Day's Pleasure, etc. 32mo 75

Thomas Hughes.

Tom Brown's School-Days at Rugby. *Illustrated Edition.* 16mo 1.00
Tom Brown at Oxford. 16mo 1.25

Henry James, Jr.

A Passionate Pilgrim, and Other Tales. 12mo . . . 2.00
Roderick Hudson. 12mo 2.00
The American. 12mo 2.00
Watch and Ward. "Little Classic" style. 18mo . 1.25
The Europeans. 12mo 1.50
Confidence. 12mo 1.50
The Portrait of a Lady. 12mo 2.00

Anna Jameson.

Studies and Stories. "Little Classic" style. 18mo . 1.50

Douglas Jerrold.

Mrs. Caudle's Curtain Lectures. Illustrated. "Riverside Classics." 16mo 1.00

Sarah Orne Jewett.

Deephaven. 16mo 1.25
Old Friends and New. 18mo 1.25
Country By-Ways. 18mo 1.25
The Mate of the Daylight. 18mo 1.25
A Country Doctor. 16mo 1.25
A Marsh Island. 16mo 1.25

Rossiter Johnson.

"Little Classics." Each in one volume. 18mo.

    I. Exile.   IV. Life.
    II. Intellect.   V. Laughter.
    III. Tragedy.   VI. Love.

VII. Romance.
VIII. Mystery.
IX. Comedy.
X. Childhood.
XI. Heroism.
XII. Fortune.
XIII. Narrative Poems.
XIV. Lyrical Poems.
XV. Minor Poems.
XVI. Nature.
XVII. Humanity.
XVIII. Authors.

 Each volume $1.00
 The set 18.00
 Half calf, or half morocco 45.00
The Same. In nine volumes, square 16mo.
 The set 13.50
 Half calf 27.00
 Tree calf 40.50
   (*Sold only in sets.*)

Charles and Mary Lamb.
Tales from Shakespeare. 18mo 1.00
The Same. Illustrated. 16mo 1.00
The Same. *Handy-Volume Edition.* 32mo, gilt top . 1.25

Henry Wadsworth Longfellow.
Hyperion. A Romance. 16mo 1.50
Popular Edition. 16mo 40
Popular Edition. Paper covers, 16mo 15
Outre-Mer. 16mo 1.50
Popular Edition. 16mo 40
Popular Edition. Paper covers, 16mo 15
Kavanagh. 16mo 1.50

S. Weir Mitchell.
In War Time. 16mo 1.25

Nora Perry.
The Tragedy of the Unexpected, and Other Stories.
"Little Classic" style. 18mo 1.25

Elizabeth Stuart Phelps.
The Gates Ajar. 16mo 1.50
Beyond the Gates. 16mo 1.25
Men, Women, and Ghosts. 16mo 1.50
Hedged In. 16mo 1.50
The Silent Partner. 16mo 1.50
The Story of Avis. 16mo 1.50
Sealed Orders, and Other Stories. 16mo 1.50
Friends: A Duet. 16mo 1.25
Doctor Zay. 16mo 1.25

Marian C. L. Reeves and Emily Read.
Pilot Fortune. 16mo 1.25

Works of Fiction Published by

Riverside Paper Series.
A Series of Novels by the best American Authors.
1. But Yet a Woman. By A. S. Hardy.
2. Missy. By the author of " Rutledge."
3. The Stillwater Tragedy. By T. B. Aldrich.
4. Elsie Venner. By O. W. Holmes.
5. An Earnest Trifler. By Mary A. Sprague.
6. The Lamplighter. By Maria S. Cummins.
7. Their Wedding Journey. By W. D. Howells.
8. Married for Fun. Anonymous.
9. An Old Maid's Paradise. By Elizabeth Stuart Phelps.
10. The House of a Merchant Prince. By W. H. Bishop.
11. An Ambitious Woman, By Edgar Fawcett.
12. Marjorie's Quest. By Jeanie T. Gould (Mrs. Lincoln).
13. Hammersmith. By Mark Sibley Severance.

Each volume, 16mo, paper covers . . . . . . $ .50

Joseph Xavier Boniface Saintine.
Picciola. " Riverside Classics." Illustrated. 16mo . 1.00

Jacques Henri Bernardin de Saint-Pierre.
Paul and Virginia. " Riverside Classics." Illustrated. 16mo 1.00
The Same, together with Undine, and Sintram. 32mo .75

Sir Walter Scott.
The Waverley Novels. *Illustrated Library Edition.* This edition has been carefully edited, and is illustrated with 100 engravings by Darley, Dielman, Fredericks, Low, Share, Sheppard, and has also a glossary and a very full index of characters. In 25 volumes, 12mo.

Waverley.
Guy Mannering.
The Antiquary.
Rob Roy.
Old Mortality.
Black Dwarf, and Legend of Montrose.
Heart of Mid-Lothian.
Bride of Lammermoor.
Ivanhoe.
The Monastery.
The Abbot.
Kenilworth.

The Pirate.
The Fortunes of Nigel.
Peveril of the Peak.
Quentin Durward.
St. Ronan's Well.
Redgauntlet.
The Betrothed, and the Highland Widow.
The Talisman, and Other Tales.
Woodstock.
The Fair Maid of Perth.
Anne of Geierstein.

Count Robert of Paris.   The Surgeon's Daughter,
                         and Castle Dangerous.
   Each volume $1.00
   The set 25.00
   Half calf 62.50
   Half seal 75.00
Globe Edition. Complete in 13 volumes. With 100 Illustrations. 16mo.
   The set 16.25
   Half calf, or half morocco 35.00
      (*Sold only in sets.*)
Tales of a Grandfather. *Illustrated Library Edition.*
With six steel plates. In three volumes, 12mo . . 4.50
   Half calf 9.00
Ivanhoe. Fancy binding. 8vo 1.00
   Half calf 2.50

Horace E. Scudder.

The Dwellers in Five-Sisters' Court. 16mo. . . . 1.25
Stories and Romances. 16mo 1.25

Mark Sibley Severance.

Hammersmith: His Harvard Days. 12mo . . . 1.50

T. D. Sherwood.

Comic History of the United States. Illustrated. 12mo 2.50

J. E. Smith.

Oakridge : An Old-Time Story of Maine. 12mo . . 2.00

Mary A. Sprague.

An Earnest Trifler. 16mo 1.25

Harriet Beecher Stowe.

Agnes of Sorrento. 12mo 1.50
The Pearl of Orr's Island. 12mo 1.50
Uncle Tom's Cabin. *Popular Illustrated Edition.*
  12mo 2.00
The Minister's Wooing. 12mo 1.50
The Mayflower, and Other Sketches. 12mo . . . 1.50
Dred. 12mo 1.50
Oldtown Folks. 12mo 1.50
Sam Lawson's Fireside Stories. Illustrated. *New Edition*, enlarged 1.50
My Wife and I. Illustrated. 12mo 1.50
We and Our Neighbors. Illustrated. 12mo . . . 1.50
Poganuc People. Illustrated. 12mo 1.50
  The above eleven volumes, in box 16.50

Works of Fiction.

Uncle Tom's Cabin. *Holiday Edition.* With red line border, Introduction, and a Bibliography by George Bullen, of the British Museum. Over 100 Illustrations. 12mo $3.50
   Half calf 6.00
   Morocco, or tree calf 7.50
Popular Edition. 12mo 1.00
A Dog's Mission, etc. Illustrated. Small 4to . . . 1.25
Queer Little People. Illustrated. Small 4to . . . 1.25
Little Pussy Willow. Illustrated. Small 4to . . . 1.25

Gen. Lew Wallace.
The Fair God; or, The Last of the 'Tzins. 12mo . 1.50

Henry Watterson.
Oddities in Southern Life and Character. Illustrated. 16mo 1.50

Richard Grant White.
The Fate of Mansfield Humphreys, together with the Episode of Mr. Washington Adams in England. 16mo 1.25

Adeline D. T. Whitney.
Faith Gartney's Girlhood. Illustrated. 12mo . . . 1.50
Hitherto: A Story of Yesterdays. 12mo 1.50
Patience Strong's Outings. 12mo 1.50
The Gayworthys. 12mo 1.50
Leslie Goldthwaite. Illustrated. 12mo 1.50
We Girls: A Home Story. Illustrated. 12mo . . 1.50
Real Folks. Illustrated. 12mo 1.50
The Other Girls. Illustrated. 12mo 1.50
Sights and Insights. 2 vols. 12mo 3.00
Odd, or Even? 12mo 1.50
Boys at Chequasset. Illustrated. 12mo 1.50
The above twelve volumes in box 18.00

⁂ For sale by all Booksellers. Sent, post-paid, on receipt of price (in check on Boston or New York, money-order, or registered letter) by the Publishers,

HOUGHTON, MIFFLIN AND COMPANY,

4 PARK ST., BOSTON, MASS.; 11 EAST SEVENTEENTH ST., NEW YORK.

A Catalogue containing portraits of many of the above authors, with a description of their works, will be sent free, on application, to any address.

www.ingramcontent.com/pod-product-compliance
Lightning Source LLC
Chambersburg PA
CBHW022101230426
43672CB00008B/1240